God Makes a Way

Susan Mbaluka

TEACH Services, Inc.
P U B L I S H I N G
www.TEACHServices.com

World rights reserved. This book or any portion thereof may not be copied or reproduced in any form or manner whatever, except as provided by law, without the written permission of the publisher, except by a reviewer who may quote brief passages in a review.

This book was written to provide truthful information in regard to the subject matter covered. The author assumes full responsibility for the accuracy of all facts and quotations as cited in this book. The opinions expressed in this book are the author's personal views and interpretation of the Bible, Spirit of Prophecy, and/or contemporary authors and do not necessarily reflect those of TEACH Services, Inc.

This book is sold with the understanding that the publisher is not engaged in giving spiritual, legal, medical, or other professional advice. If authoritative advice is needed, the reader should seek the counsel of a competent professional

Copyright © 2012 TEACH Services, Inc.
ISBN-13: 978-1-57258-689-5 (Paperback)
ISBN-13: 978-1-57258-690-1 (Hardback)
ISBN-13: 978-1-57258-691-8 (ePub)
ISBN-13: 978-1-57258-812-7 (Kindle)

Library of Congress Control Number: 2011940583

All scripture quotations are taken from the King James Version Bible.

Published by

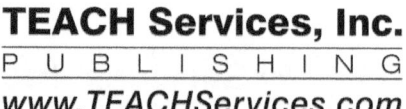

www.TEACHServices.com

Table of Contents

Chapter 1   Death Was Ever Eminent 5

Chapter 2   Blessings Disguised in a Painful Accident 13

Chapter 3   I Learned About Sabbath 22

Chapter 4   God Gave Me the Desires of My Heart 33

Chapter 5   A Wedding or Eloping at Night? 39

Chapter 6   Mystery Solved 45

Chapter 7   Miracle Deliverance 48

Chapter 8   Peace Beyond Understanding 51

Chapter 9   Trusting God Through Threats of Death 57

Chapter 10 God's Plan Was the Best 63

Chapter 11 In The Wilderness 68

Chapter 12 God Rescued Me From Satan's Attack 75

Chapter 13 Incredible Flight From Chattanooga to Houston 81

Chapter 14 Witnessing at Advent Home 85

Chapter 15 Miracle Ticket to Kenya 91

Chapter 16 Missionary Work While in Kenya 100

Chapter 17 I Was Sent to Visit a Family 107

Chapter 18 Back to the U.S. With Anxiety 112

Chapter 19 Distracted From Writing..117

Chapter 20 God Overcame for Me..123

Chapter 21 I Received a Call 129

Chapter 22 Where Are You Going From Advent Home? 135

Chapter 23 Reunited at Last..143

Chapter 1

Death Was Ever Eminent

"You were so sick and emaciated that nobody wanted to hold you even for a minute. People thought you were going to die like your older sister. Nobody wanted you to die in his or her hands. Measles almost sent you to the grave. Since you did not die as a toddler, don't worry about poisonous snakes under your bed, rhinoceros in our garden, or the witch doctors in our village. The God who sustained you while your brother and your sister died will preserve your life," my mother told me.

I felt a bit comforted, but I did not say a word. I could still remember the rhino and a calf that had passed a few meters from our grass-thatched, mud-walled hut the previous week only to get news two days later that the animal killed a man and his wife in the neighboring village.

On this day, I had been given the responsibility of making sure that the fire was kept burning under the clay pot that stood on the three stone woodstove in the middle of the hut cooking maize mixed with beans for lunch. There was a big heap of firewood outside the hut for this purpose. In addition to keeping the fire burning under the pot, I was also supposed to keep adding water to the pot whenever it was needed to ensure that the food did not burn. It was whilst doing this that I heard drums and screams from the other side of the village. On listening more keenly, I heard "*Mbusya nisu* (there comes a rhino)."

For a moment, I did not feel the smoke that ruthlessly burned my eyes. I stood at the door of the hut and called to my younger siblings who were playing outside. As the young children ran into the hut, I continued standing at the door wondering exactly where the animal was passing and at what part of the forest my older brother, Laki, was grazing our cows. I also wondered whether my mother had heard the warning from where she worked in the farm.

Suddenly, in lightning speed, Mother appeared from the jungle, the edges of her multi-colored headscarf flying in the air, and gave the hut one sweeping look with her bright eyes. She saw that we were all there apart from my older brother. Then she stood in front of the hut, her slender body giving the appearance of a warrior ready to attack, calling, "Laki, Laki!" Laki answered from the other side of the jungle.

"Climb up a tree. A rhino is coming. Do you hear?" A trumpet could not have been louder than Mother at that time.

"Yes, Mother, I'm climbing up a tree now," my brother echoed.

After two or so minutes, his voice could be heard again. "Mother, I'm at the top of a tree now."

"Stay there until I tell you to come down," Mother instructed him.

"Yes, Mother," he replied.

Once Mother ensured that her children were safe, she joined the other villagers in warning everybody in the village and the neighboring village that a rhino was coming. Within a few minutes, the rhino and a calf passed by a few meters from our hut. The huge animal walked slowly at the pace of the calf. A few minutes later, Mother came into the hut and, with a long, large wooden scoop, took some food out of the pot. It was ready and had just enough water in it. "Susana, you are diligent. The food is ready and well done. Very good," she told me. I smiled with confidence.

But that was then. This particular day, I felt different.

Up to the late 1960s, Makueni District in Kenya was mainly a jungle heavily inhabited by pythons, buffalos, rhinos, and many other dangerous wild animals roaming freely. Nobody seemed distressed by the presence of the animals; however, this day my mother noticed that I was quieter than usual.

"You look worried, Susana. What's the problem?" she asked.

"The sun is setting," I said almost in a whisper.

"Darkness doesn't bite anybody, my child. I've told you this many times. Anyway, we are about to go home. Tie your firewood together as I finish cutting this branch; then we will go in and light a fire before the sun sets completely," Mother told me.

I grabbed my rope and finished tying my firewood even before she completed cutting the branch of dry wood. I then stood in front of her begging her with my eyes to leave the pursuit of more firewood for another day.

I had a phobia of darkness even though electricity was unknown in our village. Glowing wood splints lit the whole hut at night. Although the mud walls had deep cracks, I felt much safer there at night. I did not like to put my bare feet in grass at night. All the same, on this day I was more scared of the darkness than usual. The previous night a snake had crawled under the door of our hut and had slithered under the bed that I shared with my sister. Our hens with their chicks slept under our bed. I was awakened by the hens screeching as the snake feasted on their chicks.

My sister and I were too scared to move. Normally, we would have jumped over to our mother's bed, which was on the other side of the hut, but my mother had a little child, so she could not help fight the intruder. My young brother, considering himself the only man in the house, woke up, pulled dry grass off from the side of the hut, and lit it from the cooking fire in the center of the hut. This allowed him enough light to see the red snake that had wound itself under my bed after hearing the commotion. My brother killed it by shooting it with a bow and arrow.

All this time, my mother had called on God to save us. After the snake was killed, Mother started talking as if to resuscitate us from our state of shock.

"God protects us from all dangers," she said.

We were silent. We were still in shock.

"The snakes are numerous now just because we moved here recently. After some time, you will not see so many of them in the homestead," she encouraged us. "I wish your father could come home for a few days. He would help to clear the homestead of bushes," she posed.

"Yes, Mother, I wish Father could come home, too. It's been a long time since I have seen him," I responded, my head still buried in my blankets.

"I know. It's been five years now, but he has to stay in Nairobi and work every day so that he can raise money for your brother's school fees. If he comes home, he will not be paid. Watchmen are only paid for the days they work," Mother explained.

Now that the snake was dead and the hens had quieted down, Mother encouraged us to relax and sleep. But it was not easy to fall asleep; my heart was still racing as if I had just competed in a 200-meter race in the World Games. Whenever my sister's foot touched mine, I imagined a snake had now made it to our bed. So I curled myself up as a cabbage. Poisonous snakes had killed two of my cousins and one of our dogs. I did not want to have anything to do with them.

I don't know what time I fell asleep, but the next thing I heard was Mother calling me.

"Susana, don't you fear the cane of the teacher today? Wake up, wash your face, and put on your school uniform. Your porridge will be ready in a minute."

I woke up at once, glanced at the steaming pot of porridge, and taking water in a calabash, went out of the hut and poured the water in a basin to wash my face and legs. I bathed completely on the weekends or on some evenings. Even though I did not take a full bath on a daily basis, I knew I was clean. After all, the previous week a lady teacher at school had announced in front of the class, "Susana's face is brighter than other children's."

By the time I entered the hut, Mother had poured the porridge into a half gourd and cooled it enough for me to gulp it in a few minutes. My lunch, usually maize mixed with beans, our staple food, was packed in a bowl that had an improvised cover and was tied tightly with a piece of cloth so that even if the bowl fell as I ran through the forest the food would not spill. I put on my school uniform: a green khaki dress and a yellow blouse that I wore under the short-sleeved dress. Primary school students did not wear shoes to school, and in any case, I had never owned any. After gulping my porridge, I grabbed the packed food and stormed out of the hut walking as fast as my tender legs could carry me. Whenever we were late, the teacher would discipline us with his cane as if we were wild animals infected with rabies.

"Which route should I take?" I asked Mom.

"Go through the forest so that you get to school on time," she told me.

"I'm afraid of the forest," I retorted.

"My child, the rhinos and buffalos have not been seen anywhere in our village for a while. The hunters have killed them all. Besides, God will go with you. What are you afraid of?" she questioned.

"Crawling things." I did not want to mention their name.

"Oh, you are still thinking about last night's snake. All right, take whichever path you like," she told me.

"I will take the main path. The sun is not up yet, so it must be early. I will not be late," I said as I disappeared. I wished that my younger sisters were old enough to go with me to school.

Taking the forest route meant walking for seven miles through one long mass of tall grass, bushes, and trees. Although rhinos and buffalos were rare in the district by the time I started going to school, pythons often swallowed dogs and goats, and poisonous snakes killed people. And besides, my childhood memories of the rhinos and buffalos were still fresh in my mind. However, the idea of God protecting us from all dangers, as Mom told us repeatedly, was comforting.

My mother's faith in God and her courage kept me going. Her fortitude gave me strength to go to school even though witches and witchdoctors spread scary concoctions and dead birds along my path. Mother would tell me, "You are not a devil worshipper. You have nothing to do with their sacrifices; just walk over their concoctions and go to school."

It was believed that the witches and witchdoctors transferred sicknesses and misfortunes to the dead birds and other sacrifices and then took the sacrifices to the road to pass on to another person. It was believed that the first person to walk over the sacrifices picked up the sickness or misfortune transferred to the sacrifice. Our neighbor was a famous witchdoctor. Many people visited him to be treated so that they could not be bewitched or to undo bewitching and misfortunes that were on them. People bitten by mosquitoes would often develop a high fever and chills from malaria, but they would think they had been bewitched. They would then rush to the witchdoctor to be treated. Many times malaria and other diseases killed people because they visited the witchdoctors instead of seeking proper treatment. But these doctors were more trusted than the hospital in the area, which was a five-hour walk from our village. Because of superstition, people traveling very early in the morning would turn back and cancel their trips to avoid walking over the concoctions and sacrifices on the road.

Normally, the paths were very narrow and along the sides ran big thorny fences to keep cows and other domestic animals from straying into other people's gardens or property. Since I had to walk very early in the morning to cover the seven miles to school before 8:00 a.m., I had no choice but to walk over the sacrifices, which were mostly placed at night or in the wee hours of the morning.

Mother frequently reminded me that sicknesses and misfortunes would not come upon me just because I walked over evil sacrifices. She told me that God protected Christians. Looking back now, I know that Mother had very little knowledge about God. She had been in contact with some missionaries long before she married my father and had converted to Christianity. Her parents had been converted, too. That is how she was able to have a firm faith in God in the midst of so many heathens. However, she was still a baby in Christianity.

I saw Matthew 17:20 fulfilled in her: "And Jesus said unto them, Because of your unbelief: for verily I say unto you, If ye have faith as a grain of mustard seed, ye shall say unto this mountain, Remove hence to yonder place; and it shall remove; and nothing shall be impossible unto you." Mother's little faith was able to inspire confidence and peace in my siblings and me when most other people in our village lived in fear of contracting diseases or having misfortunes fall upon them from walking over some natural plants mixed with animal blood.

The kind of darkness we had in our village in the sixties and the seventies is rare in most parts of the world today. However, Satan still uses the same principles. People still hold beliefs that are Satan's lies to enslave them. "God hath dealt to every man the measure of faith" (Rom. 12:3). What we do with that faith will determine whether we, as Christians, will be able to stand firm for God even if the heavens fall.

Even though Mother only completed grade three in school, she wanted her children to become teachers. The most educated, most respected person, the one who had the best lifestyle in the village, was a teacher. And though teachers were extremely rare in those days, Mother had seen them in her district, Mbooni, where she had come in contact with missionaries. She knew something better than the poverty, superstition, disease, and ignorance she experienced in the village.

Makueni District was notorious for droughts. Once droughts hit, farmers went hungry and their children dropped out of school. Professionals like teachers had a salary. They could always buy food. Mother wanted us to have better lives and a future. That is why she was able to transcend the cultural belief of the day that educating a girl was a waste of time and resources; she educated all five of her daughters.

Nothing could stop Mother from working toward her vision. Even though Dad was totally illiterate, Mother was able to inspire him enough to leave home and go to the city of Nairobi to get a job as a watchman in order to pay for our education.

At the time Dad left home, our house was on a fifty-acre farm. The homestead was clear of bushes and long grass, but the house was next to the main path in the village, and there was a lot of disturbance from passersby, especially drunkards. Some of these men would walk for miles looking for traditional brew. After drinking themselves almost to a crawling position, they would stagger back to the village late at night. On reaching the village, some would start calling the names of their wives at the top of their voices. Others would yell insults at their enemies in the village. Therefore, in pursuit of security, peace, and privacy, Mother, with the help of a hired man in the village, moved deeper into the jungle and put up a simple hut for our family.

Years passed quickly; soon I was in standard seven, and it was time to sit for the C.P.E. (Certificate of Primary Education). This was the final exam at the completion of primary (elementary) education; this was a national exam that all the children in Kenya wrote at the end of standard seven (the equivalent of grade eight). The exam was set by the Ministry of Education. Children who performed well were admitted to secondary (high) schools. There were so few secondary schools in Kenya that there were not enough slots for everyone who completed elementary school. Hence, the examination was an elimination tool. A few of the young people in our village who had made it to standard seven sought supernatural powers from witch doctors in order to pass the exam. The kids who visited the witch doctors were either given some traditional medicines tied tightly in a piece of cloth to carry with them (especially on the days of the exam) or deep cuts on their skin with black powder rubbed on the cuts or both. At school we saw these marks, and our peers told us why they had them. A few days before our exam, I reported these happenings to my mother.

In response, she confidently told me, "Your supernatural powers come from the God of Abraham and Isaac. We will pray for you every day. That will

God Makes a Way

be your empowering potion."

I relaxed. The exam came at last. We sat for it, and then we had to wait one month for the results.

I wonder how I would have felt if, as we waited for the results, Mom would have read Philippians 4:6, 7 to me: "Be careful for nothing; but in every thing by prayer and supplication with thanksgiving let your requests be made known to God. And the peace of God, which passeth all understanding, shall keep your hearts and minds through Christ Jesus."

Chapter 2

Blessings Disguised in a Painful Accident

The month that had seemed endless came to an end. Our final elementary exam results were out. Although the exam was set and marked by a national body under the Ministry of Education, when the results were out, they were sent to every school. It was during that time when all the former candidates rushed to school to find out how they had performed. I was the only one who passed from my village. I wished I had wings to fly back home to tell my mother and my siblings.

"I told you; a witch doctor is not God. Now praise God," Mother told me.

Nothing strengthened my faith in God more than this experience. While we were talking and praising God, my aunt, who is our neighbor, passed by on her way to the market.

"What's happening to Susana today? Her milk white teeth are all exposed today! Why are you so happy, girl?" my aunt asked.

"She just got her C.P.E. results from school. The girl did well in her exam. I pray that God will provide the means for us to take her to high school," Mother said.

"Very good. I was wondering why she had problems keeping her lips together," my aunt joked. We all roared with laughter.

"She looks like she's already in high school. Her light skin glows more today. And look at her short black kinky hair neatly combed and shining than ever before," my aunt said. I grinned shyly.

"She had to go for her results looking neat. But now she needs to change clothes and rush to the river for water," instructed Mom.

After the results were out, we had to wait for about two weeks to receive admission letters to secondary schools. One day, when we least expected, we heard a voice call out. "Anybody home?" It was our neighbor.

"Welcome," Mother replied from our hut. After exchanging greetings, the man handed Mother two letters.

"I was given these letters by the head teacher of Matulani Primary School. He told me they are for Susana," the man said.

Although five of us children were in the hut with Mother, we listened to the conversation but acted as if we did not hear anything. Culture forbade children to interrupt grown-up talk or concern themselves with their parents' business. However, I almost broke this taboo when they mentioned my name. I fidgeted on my stool as I gazed at the two letters.

"Here, read and tell me where they came from," Mother told me.

I received invitation letters to two different girls' boarding schools, but boarding schools were more expensive than day schools. My father's watchman salary could not cover boarding school fees for my elder brother and me. In order to keep both of us in high school, my parents decided to send me to Nairobi to live with my father and attend school in the city as a day scholar. Having grown-up in a rural village, my father took me to the city center to show me the school and instruct me on how to cross streets and take public transport to the outskirts of the city where he lived in the Kawangware slum.

On alighting at the city center, Father took me to Ravals Secondary School. The principal gladly enrolled me in form one. However, I had to go back with Dad that day so that he could show me the stage from where I would be taking buses from school back to Kawangware. From the school, we walked for a while, crossing a few streets.

Before crossing any street, Dad would stop and tell me, "Look! When you come here, stop and check both sides of the street to make sure there are no vehicles coming. Then cross." This was 1977, and the vehicles in the streets of Nairobi then were nothing comparable to what we have today. There were very few vehicles then. Just the same, Dad did not take anything for granted. We stopped at every street whether there was a vehicle in sight or not.

After walking for some time, Dad stopped talking to me. He seemed to be lost in his thoughts, and he was walking fast. I quietly but briskly kept pace with him. As a girl, I had been taught to talk to my father only when it was absolutely necessary. We walked side by side until we came to a particular street where Dad walked straight across without stopping to check for oncoming vehicles. Earlier, he had told me that I had to stop and check both ways before crossing. But as I stopped at this street, he kept going. I had no chance to call him or pull him back.

Then it happened. In a fraction of a second, I saw a big army lorry roll by and then stop suddenly in front of me. For a few seconds, I could not see Dad. Then I saw him under the huge lorry.

There were two army men on the lorry. I did not know how many were in the driver's cabin. The two of them at the back climbed down and quickly loaded Dad into the vehicle. By this time, Father was unconscious. One of them helped me climb in. I cannot find words to explain the shock, fear, and pain I felt at the time. For about thirty minutes, I cried, calling my dad's name, but he could not hear. I tried to touch him to see if he could feel. Then I noticed that his right arm was completely broken between the shoulder and the elbow. The arm was badly twisted toward his back. I took it and put it back in place and held it there until we reached the hospital.

All this time, I was crying and asking the men, "*Mwikinyaa Nau niki?*" ("Why did you hit father?") The army men were quiet. One of them told me they did not do it on purpose.

They took us to Kenyatta National Hospital. Once there, they lied to the nurses, telling them that Dad was a victim of a hit-and-run accident. They said they had picked him up from the street. After saying their piece, they left us at the hospital. I did not understand Swahili well. Having grown up in a village where there were no vehicles, I did not even know that I should've written down the number of the license plate and told the truth about the accident. In any case, I had been too busy holding Dad's arm in place to think about anything else.

Dad was put on a stretcher and was kept there for a while before someone attended to him. I stood beside him and cried the whole time. After some time, he opened his eyes and saw me. He told me, "Don't cry. I will be well."

Thank God he is not dead, I thought. I felt life coming back to me after I saw him open his eyes. My shock started fading away. I don't know how long I stood beside my dad before nurses came for him. Kenyatta National Hospital was the biggest and most developed hospital in East and Central Africa. All the cases that could not be handled in provincial hospitals in Kenya were referred to this enormous hospital. People from other African countries were also brought to Kenyatta Hospital because of its modern and sophisticated equipment. As a result, there were always too many people to attend to.

I remained outside when the nurses took Dad in for examination. It was then that I looked around. I saw people in worse conditions than my dad. Some were accident victims. Others were too sick to recognize themselves. I felt comforted that Dad was not that sick. However, I quietly continued praying to God to heal him.

After several hours in the hospital, he was discharged. I was very happy to see him walk out of the hospital. However, he was still confused, and he could not remember what route we needed to take to go back to the estate. He could not even walk straight. I supported him although he was over six feet tall and I was about five feet. We somehow found our way to the bus station, but he could not remember what bus number went to Kawangware where he lived. I had two maternal uncles in Kawangware, but there were no telephones anywhere near where we lived, and I wouldn't have known how to use a telephone even if I had had access to one. The only person I could call upon was God. I kept praying in my heart all the time I was struggling to keep Dad from falling.

After a few minutes of this torture in the bus station, I saw Dad's neighbor. He seemed to appear out of nowhere. On seeing me struggling with Dad, he came running and took Dad by the arm. He did not even tell us where he was going. He asked us if we wanted to go back to the slum where Dad lived. On saying yes, he took us on a bus and sat with Dad to support him. He took us up to Dad's hovel. This is one of the many miracles that God performed in my life.

That evening I thought Father was going to die. His broken arm had only been wrapped with a bandage, no plaster, and he did not have any painkillers. I had never seen a person in so much pain in my life. It was only the two of us in the hovel. Mom was very far away in the village with the rest of the children. My elder brother was in a boarding school in a different district. Since there were no telephones in the village, I wrote a letter to Mom and gave it to my uncles to give to anybody going to the village or send by bus to the nearest market in our village. I was extremely traumatized, but Dad and I prayed every day to God to heal him. By this time, Dad was over sixty years old and recovery was slow. And he had no insurance for proper treatment.

To make matters worse, he was a casual worker, a watchman; so now that he was not working, he could not get any money from work. He had no savings, but food had to be bought. For a few days we survived on porridge until the flour ran out.

"Susana, do you remember where I took you to my small garden along the river near Lavington Center?" Dad asked me.

"Yes, Dad," I said.

"Go there and cut some cassava leaves and bring them to me. We will cook them to eat with *ugali* (thick cornmeal). Your uncle James gave me a little money for flour, but we cannot afford to buy vegetables in the market. Walk on the left side of the road and remember to check the streets very carefully before you cross," Father instructed me.

I walked the few miles to Dad's small garden at "no man's land" along the river banks and cut as much cassava leaves as I could get. I came back praying that we would not die from these leaves; I had never seen anybody eat cassava leaves before.

One and a half months later, Mother arrived with some grain from the village.

This accident marked the end of my high school education for that year. By this time, my elder brother, Jackson (Laki), was doing his form four in high school. Form four was the equivalent to twelfth grade. The little money my mother earned from selling surplus food and chickens went to pay for my brother's school fees so that he could graduate from high school. I had to drop out of school.

However, to me, education was as important as life itself. I remembered the promise I had made to Mom when I was in standard four (grade 4) that when I grew up she would not go hungry or wear rags as she did. Now my hopes were dashed.

I cried every day until one day my father told me, "Susana, you have cried for a very long time. You have been so sad for so long; this sadness can make you sick. Why do you cry like this? I was ready to take you to school; I will still educate you. Keep yourself like a school girl. I am still alive; just be patient and wait for me to recover and go back to work. I will educate you till you get tired of school. Do not cry anymore."

Since that day, I had hope. I respected my father's word. Dad had made a promise to me, and I knew it was a matter of time before I would go back to school. Therefore, I stopped focusing on the fact that I had dropped out of school and instead focused on praying for Dad to recover, go back to work, and take me back to school.

After several months, Dad went back to work. As a watchman, he worked at night, so I spent nights alone in the hovel since Mother had gone back to the village after one month of nursing Dad. The hovels were single mud-walled rooms with iron sheet roofs. One plot accommodated many tenants with more than 90 percent of the residents being men. A few days after Dad went back to work, one evening I heard a knock on the door. Dad had already left for work.

I asked, "Who is knocking?"

"Mwanzia," a voice answered.

Without thinking, I opened the door. The young man came straight for my neck and choked me as he pushed me to the only bed in the room. I did not waste time. I tightened the muscles around my neck and reached for his neck, strangling him harder than he was strangling me. We struggled for a few minutes before he realized that instead of achieving his mission he was going to get terribly hurt. He gave up and left, but he left bruises and marks on my brown skin, especially around the neck. I thanked God for giving me strength and protecting me from rape and possible murder.

The following day my father came early in the morning as usual. Before reaching our room, a neighbor met him on the way and told him that there had been somebody in our room the previous night. After a few hours of my silence, Dad realized I did not plan to tell him anything about the incident. He asked me, "Who came here after I went to work?"

"Mwanzia," I said.

"What did he want?" asked Dad.

"He did not tell me," I answered.

Mwanzia was a son of Dad's friend, a fellow watchman. The tall, thin, weak-looking boy was a student in one of the secondary schools in the city. I knew him and his father from passing by our place and saying hello. Since both our fathers worked at night, he knew I was alone in the room.

"All right, prepare yourself. I am going to send you to the village to stay there and wait for this year to end so that you can join school at the beginning of next year. Go home and help your mother with work for the remaining few months," Father told me.

"Yes, Father," I said.

As I washed my clothes to prepare for my trip home, I did not know whether to be happy or sad because as much as I wanted to live with Dad, the life was both dangerous and lonely. There was no electricity in the plot, no running water or radio (I did not know televisions existed.) There were no other girls for me to talk to. But I liked fetching water from the tap outside the plot and cooking for Dad. I was my father's favorite child, but now that he had decided to send me to the village, I had mixed feelings. All the same, I went home.

In the village, I helped Mother by fetching water on my back from the river, collecting firewood from the forest, herding cattle, weeding the farm, cooking, and taking care of my younger siblings. Although the year had seemed long at the beginning, it passed quickly. Toward the end of the year, Mother told me that she wanted me to go to a boarding school. She mentioned a school in the district where most of the girls who had joined high school from our region had gone.

"Even if education was free there, I would not like to go to that school," I told Mother.

"Why?" she asked.

"All the girls I know who went there have dropped out of school because they became pregnant, and the only one who completed form four did not get a high school certificate. She failed the K.C.S.E. (Kenya Certificate of Secondary Education, the final national high school exam)," I said.

"Okay, I will take you to Mutitu Seventh-day Adventist Secondary School where your cousins are going to school. It is a boarding school. All you will do with your time there is to study seriously," Mother told me.

This school was one day's journey on a bus from our village. My cousins whom my mom had said were attending the school were almost strangers to me because I had seen them only once. They lived in another location that was more civilized than ours. They lived in Mbooni location, one of the places where missionaries were stationed first in Ukambani. Mutitu SDA Secondary School was within walking distance from their home. I did not know much about this school, but I was very excited about it.

I wanted a school far from the village. Mom secured admission for me, but there was no money for school fees. We kept praying, and somehow by the reporting date, Mom had earned enough money by selling a calf and some maize to pay for me to start school.

The day I put on my school uniform and walked into the classroom, I felt as if I had reached heaven. To the other students it was just another school, but for me, it was a miracle. Here I did not have to spend nights alone in a city slum and face the danger of rape and murder. I had security here. In this boarding school, we had a generator that gave us lights to study in the evenings. Compared to the city school, I had time to concentrate on my studies instead of fetching water, cooking, and getting distracted by noise from other hovels in the plot.

Mutitu means forest in my mother tongue, and sure enough our school was in the forest. This was the perfect environment for learning. For the first time, I had a bed to myself. Our dormitory was a long rectangular building made of burned bricks on the walls and cemented floor with iron sheets on the roof. Our matron made sure that our rooms were thoroughly cleaned and neatly kept. I had never lived in a cement-floored house before. Our classrooms were built with the same materials as the dormitories. Also, I liked the fact that there were cooks to cook for us. Therefore, I had a chance to spend the whole day in class and to participate in games with other students. At home, I had very little time for recreation. The teachers in this Adventist school did not call us names like those in public primary school. I liked everything about this Adventist school.

In addition, we had worship in the morning and evening every day. Nothing made me happier. Within one week, I forgot all the crying and pain I had gone through while waiting to go to school. Although I became very homesick after a month or so, I was so glad that I did not join the school in the city. With all the dangers of having to be by myself every night, I could not see myself completing high school.

Whenever my memories flashback to that time, I can't help but think about Romans 8:28: "And we know that all things work together for good to them that love God, to them who are the called according to his purpose."

After Dad's accident, I kept asking myself why God had not protected my father as my mother had always told us He would. But up to this day, I still thank God for the blessings I received through my father's painful accident.

Chapter 3

I Learned About Sabbath

At Mutitu Adventist School, I put all my effort into my studies. However, whenever I took a Bible test, I performed poorly. Yet, the girl who sat next to me in class, Agnes, always made straight As in Bible. After several frustrating tests, I decided to ask Agnes the secret behind her success.

"How do you manage to get such high points in the Bible tests?" I asked her.

"I have been studying the Bible since I learned how to read in grade three, and every Sabbath afternoon we have Bible study in my church. So, I already know the Bible stories we read in class," she told me.

"I have also been going to church while at home, and we read the Bible, too. In fact, before I came to the boarding school, I was a Sunday school teacher."

"Oh, so you are a Sundaykeeper? Why do you go to church on Sunday?" Agnes asked.

"Well, people should go to church on Sunday. It is strange to go to church on Saturday," I said.

At that point, Agnes pulled out her Bible from her desk and started reading to me. She started with Genesis 2:2, 3: "And on the seventh day God ended his work which he had made; and he rested on the seventh day from all his work which he had made. And God blessed the seventh day, and sanctified it: because that in it he had rested from all his work which God created and made." Next, she turned to Exodus 20:8-10 and read, "Remember the sabbath day, to keep it holy. Six days shalt thou labour, and do all thy work: But the seventh day is the sabbath of the LORD thy God: in it thou shalt not do any work, thou, nor thy son, nor thy daughter, thy manservant, nor thy maidservant, nor thy cattle, nor thy stranger that is within thy gates."

"Yes, God rested on the seventh day, and he wants us to do the same, and Sunday is the seventh day," I interrupted.

Agnes paused, looked at me, and calmly said, "The Bible will tell us which is the seventh day of the week." Then she opened Matthew 28:1 and read, "In the end of the sabbath, as it began to dawn the first day of the week, came Mary Magdalene and the other Mary to see the sepulchre."

Agnes continued to explain, "Jesus was crucified on Friday, and He remained in the grave on Sabbath; then he resurrected early in the morning the first day of the week. Sunday is the first day of the week." Agnes went on and on, telling me many things about the Sabbath. What amazed me most about her was how she could recite the verses from her head. She did not have to search for the verses talking about the Sabbath.

Every day this form one (grade 9) classmate taught me about the Sabbath. She also taught me a bit of prophecy as she explained to me the mark of the beast in Revelation 13:18. In addition, the school chaplain taught us about the Sabbath, too. However, Agnes made more of an impact on me than the school chaplain. In any case, the chaplain had limited time to teach me unlike Agnes who was both my classmate and my roommate. She gave me a Bible study everywhere at school.

Most of the time, I defended my faith. The only problem was that I did not know Bible verses to support going to church on Sunday, while Agnes opened the Bible to support her arguments all the time. As time went by, I stopped arguing with her and just listened to what she had to say. It took me one and a half years to make up my mind to become a Seventh-day Adventist. Toward the end of form two (10th grade), I joined the baptismal class; then in form three (11th grade), I was baptized.

When I went home on a holiday after being baptized, I asked my mother, "Mom, will you please let me go to church on Saturday?"

"There is nobody in church on Saturday. What are you going to do in church on Saturday?" she asked.

"I mean the Seventh-day Adventist church, not the Sunday church where we have been going," I told her.

"Why do you want to go to that church?" she asked in surprise.

"I was baptized into the Adventist church at school," I said. "And I would like to go to the SDA church at Muusini whenever I am home on the holidays." In those days, churches were built in shopping centers. The Adventist church was at one center while the Sunday church that my family attended was at another. Our home was in between these two shopping centers. My family hardly went to the center where the Adventist church was built because whatever we needed from the shops or from the market we bought on Sundays after church. Therefore, in spite of the fact that I wanted to go to a different denomination on my own, and on Saturday, it sounded strange that I wanted to go to church in this particular place.

"Susana, you went to Mutitu Adventist School to get an education, not to be converted to the faith. You can only go to an SDA church when you are at school. But when you come home, you will go to church with the family. On Sunday, go to church with your siblings," Mother told me.

I told her I only wanted to go to the SDA church, and if she would not allow me to go then, I would like to stay at home on the two days. On Saturday I would only study the Bible, but on Sunday I would do any work that she gave me.

Mother kept quiet but gave me a stern look. I could see in her face that she was fed up with the conversation, and I knew if I pressed her further she would explode. I neither wanted to quarrel nor did I want to be caned. I kept quiet, but deep down in my heart I was determined to go to church on the following Sabbath. I decided to wait for Saturday morning when I would go to her and ask, "Mother, may I go to church?"

However, to my shock, on Friday afternoon as Mom, Ngina, my baby sister, and I sat outside our hut peeling peas to cook, the Sunday church pastor appeared at our homestead. His home was at the other end of the village, a one-hour walk away. I had never seen him at our home. *What brought him here today?* I wondered as I went into the hut to get him a chair. After exchanging the usual greetings, Mother told me that the pastor had come to talk to me. She told me this as she took the basket of pigeon peas and my little sister to the hut where they sat throughout his visit.

It then dawned on me the mission of the pastor.

"How are you, my daughter?" he began.

"I am fine; thank you, pastor," I responded.

"How are you doing at school?

"Well," I said.

"Eh, do they force you to get converted to the Seventh-day Adventist faith?" he inquired.

"No, they don't," I told him.

"Then why did you get baptized in their church?" he asked me.

"I learned that people are supposed to keep the Sabbath day holy, so they should go to church on Saturday to worship God," I told him.

"Who taught you that?" he wanted to know.

"My classmate, our school chaplain, and other people," I told him. At this point, I asked him if I could go to the hut to get my Bible. My big brother, with the help of other young men in the village, had helped build a bigger hut with two rooms, one bedroom for my mom and my little sister and another room for my other three sisters and me. It was in our shared room that I kept a wooden box with my schoolbooks and a Bible.

I returned to the pastor, and he started telling me, "Jesus resurrected on Sunday, and on Sunday we go to church to worship a risen Savior."

"Then what does this verse mean?" I asked. I read him Matthew 5:17. "Think not that I am come to destroy the law, or the prophets: I am not come to destroy but to fulfill."

"Is that why you want to go to the SDA church?" he asked me.

"There are many verses that cause me to want to go to church on Saturday. For instance, Genesis 2:2, 3 and Exodus 20:8-10, where God instructs us to remember the Sabbath and keep it holy. Can you explain these verses to me?" I asked him.

He did not explain any verses to me. Instead, he told me, "Your mother, your father, and everyone in your family go to church on Sunday. Nobody in the whole village goes to church on Saturday. How will you, young girl, start something strange in the whole village?" he asked me.

"I'm just following what the Bible says," I responded.

Wow! I held my breath. I thought he was going to slap me in the face. Holding his Bible tightly, he shot up from his chair as if he had been stung by a bee. He headed for the door of the hut where Mother was cooking supper, announcing to her as he passed, "I'm going my way. This talk will not help anybody." Mother thanked him and bade him goodbye. He left.

Mom did not need to ask any questions. She had listened to the whole discussion from the hut. I consciously entered the kitchen and quietly sat on a three-legged stool opposite her, keeping the cooking place between us so that I could watch as she stirred a big pot of *ugali* (thick, firm cornmeal) in the middle of the hut. The whole hut was full of an appetizing aroma of fried food. By this time she was done cooking the pigeon peas in a clay pot that resembled a giraffe without legs. The pot had a big round stomach with a narrow long neck and a wide round mouth that was covered with a small dry gourd. She had boiled the pilled peas until they were tender; then she fried them together with tomatoes. She was always very meticulous in her cooking. She insisted that food had to be tasty. I could see in her face that she was unhappy about the incident between the pastor and me. I decided not to say anything unless she initiated the talk. However, I quietly helped her cook by keeping the cooking fire burning, adding more firewood as the need arose.

"Mother, look! My pot has fallen apart! Look!" Ngina lamented.

Ngina's toy clay pot that she had put on an imaginary fire at the farthest corner of the hut to cook for her maize cob toy baby had disintegrated the minute she had put water in it.

"Oh, I'm sorry. What will your child eat?" Mother responded.

"Your clay pots don't fall apart when you cook, Mother. How come?" Ngina asked.

"I thoroughly burn my pots with fire before I start cooking in them. That's why they don't disintegrate when I pour water in them, but I don't want you to handle fire because it will burn you together with your pot," Mother warned Ngina.

"I want to cook for my baby," Ngina insisted.

"Your baby has no mouth and no stomach," I teased her.

"Ahaa!" she opened her mouth to cry.

"OK. OK. I'm sorry," I apologized.

"Make another pot, and let it dry completely. Then I will burn it for you. It will hold your food, but if you drop it hard, it will break. You have to handle it with care," Mother instructed her. Ngina thanked Mom and carried her toy baby outside to look at the calves and kids in the homestead.

By the time Mom and I finished cooking, the sun was setting and my siblings started coming home from their various activities. Some of my sisters brought firewood from the forest while the others came from the river where they had gone for water. My younger brother, Ngao, brought in the cows from the jungle where they had been grazing. The silence that had dominated the homestead ceased as kids and calves ran for their mothers. The calves and cows went, *mooing* while the goats and the kids made their own noises. The young animals stayed in the homestead as the older animals went deep into the forest for food and drinking water. Evening was a reunion for both the animals and humans.

Once all the animals were in their fenced area, Mother prepared to milk the cows. "Give the kids to their mothers," she instructed my brother. Then turning to me she said, "Warm the stew and start dishing up the food for everybody. Let the children eat before they start dozing. I want to start milking the cows now so that I can finish before it is too dark to see." All I needed to do was to heap huge lumps of *ugali* in plates or in half gourds and put stew in different half gourds. Then I had to clear the kitchen so as to create space for the children to sit in twos to share the food. After washing their hands and praying, the joyous moment would start. Peacefully, each child would cut a piece of *ugali*, dip it in the stew, and eat.

I sat near the cooking place to ensure that the glowing wood kept burning to light the whole hut for all of us to see our food. I was glad the cooking place was at the center of the hut. This made it easier to light the whole hut. The firewood illuminated the hut better than our old lamp that hardly had paraffin. Men and big boys ate from their *thome*, a small hut where men lit fires and sat in the evenings talking to their grown sons or other men. Since my father and big brother were not home, I did not need to take food to their *thome*. And although mothers did not share plates with children, they ate from the kitchen with young children and their daughters.

After the day the pastor talked to me, I remained at home on Sundays as the rest of my family went to church because mother refused to let me go to the SDA church on Saturdays. On Sabbaths I took a sisal sack and my Bible and disappeared to the farm where I sat under a tree almost the whole day reading my Bible. School holidays were no longer enjoyable. I now looked forward to the opening days of school when I would go to church on Sabbaths. After two holidays of staying at home without going to church, my father told my mother to let me go to the SDA church.

Father said, "So long as in the Adventist church they worship the God of heaven, I don't care. I cannot raise a pagan child just because she does not want to go to church on Sunday."

Permission to go to church on Saturday came with a lot of trials. Saturday was the day that people worked on the farms, fetched water, collected firewood, took clothes to the river to wash, or took maize to the grinding machines to make flour for the family. To accomplish all of this, parents relied on their children's help, and they took advantage of Saturdays because children did not go to school then. My mother reminded me of all that as the reasons why I should not go to church on Saturday. Then she told me, "If you have to go to church on Saturday, you need to wake up very early in the morning, go to the farm, and work for at least two hours before you go to church."

I told her, "Mother, people do not go to work on their farms before they go to church. In Exodus 20 the Bible tells us that on that day we should not do any work. So we should not go to the river to fetch water or go to the forest to collect firewood or do any other work."

"I don't understand you anymore. If you don't want to go to the farm, carry at least six kilos of maize to the grinders and bring us flour for next week. Take the maize to the machine before you go to church. By the time you finish your worship, the flour will be ready," she told me.

Mother was telling me this because the grinding machine was at the marketplace. The marketplace was about a two-hour walk from our home. The SDA church was next to the marketplace. But I did not want to carry maize on my back to the machine on Sabbath. But if it was not taking maize to the grinder on Sabbath, it would be Mother sending me to buy salt or tomatoes or some cooking oil from the shops after church service. I understood her reasoning—the shops were also at the market, and people were too busy working on the farms to let two individuals from the same family go to the market on the same day. Now that I was going to church in the same shopping center, she thought

I should kill two birds with one stone. However, I did not want to buy stuff on Sabbath. On the other hand, I did not want to keep on disappointing her every Sabbath; so I thought of a plan.

On Sabbaths I woke up before anybody else got out of bed. I bathed quickly and left even before eating breakfast. Then I took a long route to church, going through another village where there was an Adventist family. I would go to that family and wait for them to prepare themselves after which we went to church together. After the service, I joined them again so that I could reach home when the sun was setting, because if I got home before the sun set, I was sent either to the river to fetch water or to the forest to cut firewood. Sabbath was not known in my village. In fact, there were very few Seventh-day Adventists in the whole district, so to many I looked very strange.

People also looked at me strangely because of how I celebrated Christmas. On December 25 people went to church to celebrate the birth of Christ. After Bible readings and other services, people would go to the marketplaces or to the shops next to the church and get sodas or eat whatever they pleased with their friends. Young people would get a chance to talk with their friends, especially those of the opposite sex. People did not work on this day apart from looking after cows and cooking.

On Christmas days, no services were conducted in our Adventist church. We went to church on January 1 to thank God for the new year. Therefore, on Christmas, I stayed home and cooked for the family. Many people, including my elder brother, wondered who would ever marry me because I never went out to meet other young people, but I was not bothered by people's expectations of me. By God's grace, I remained firm in my faith. I accepted the position of being strange, almost weird as far as some family members and the community was concerned. I always joked with my close friends at school that it was good to be a mystery to society.

I cannot thank God enough for leading me to Christianity at an early age. Becoming a serious Christian helped me in many ways—it gave me a reason to stay out of a lot of mischief and remain focused on my studies. Soon Bible became my best subject, and my grades in other subjects improved too. In addition, throughout my childhood I had anger issues, and I used to physically fight with people. This was a very bad thing for a girl, especially when I fought boys. Many people in the village said I would never get a husband because I fought with men. I did not like this reputation.

On becoming a serious Christian, I prayed that God would help me to stop fighting. Unfortunately, during my high school days I got into two fights, but I did not give up praying to God to take away the spirit of fighting that was within me. The last time I did fight, I fought with a young man who wanted to bully my sister and me. The talk that went round in the village scared me. So I determined in my heart that I would never fight again. I earnestly prayed to God to take away my anger. And He did. Since December 1981 to date, I have never fought with anyone.

My faith also kept me out of trouble with boys. Many girls my age did not complete their secondary school course because they either became pregnant or dropped out of school to get married at an early age.

Furthermore, Christianity made me disciplined enough to be made the school head girl. This was at the Adventist school where there were approximately 800 students. This taught me responsibility. The environment and circumstances contributed to my performing very well in the K.C.S.E. (Kenya Certificate of Secondary Education). This was the final exam in order to graduate from secondary school (grade 12). As a result, I was admitted to form five in one of the best girls' high schools in the country.

But my parents were financially drained. Yet, in spite of the financial hardships, I wanted to continue to 'A' levels (pre-university). My parents told me that they could not afford continuing my education. I prayed to God with all my heart, mind, and strength to provide for my parents. My teachers at the Adventist school encouraged me, especially the principal, Jacob Kioko, and deputy, Stephen Muasya. Mr. Muasya gave me 200 Ksh. to show to my parents and tell them to add more and take me to school. After my father saw the little money from my teachers, he decided to do whatever it took to get me to form five.

However, my grandfather and some elders in the village went to Dad and told him it was sheer foolishness to continue selling cows to educate a woman. "Susana should get married and settle down like other young women. She is not a man; why do you work so hard in Nairobi only to throw the money away in the name of paying school fees for a girl? Why does your wife keep selling cows for her fees?" they asked.

Although I did not know much about fasting, I refused to eat—my sole focus was prayer. I held on to God by faith and refused to let go until I was taken to school. Then one day, my father called me to Nairobi and told me, "I have decided to take you to school. Get all the required documents." My father does not read or write, so he could not help me gather the needed documents. However, he knew the offices where I needed to go for each document. He took me to all the offices and told me to tell the officers what I needed. He stood beside me and let me make my requests. I managed to collect all the required documents.

The problem was with the items we were required to buy. I needed at least three pairs of bed sheets, two blankets, two school uniforms, night dresses, etc., etc. We could not afford to buy even a quarter of the items. In fact, I did not even have one pair of bed sheets, a towel, or a night dress. My high school girlfriend Josephine had been called to the same school to join form five with me. She had bought everything required, and she gave me a pair of bed sheets and a towel. As for a night dress, I did not take off my school uniform until the lights were turned off. I operated like this until my father raised enough money to buy me some of the things I needed most.

On the reporting date, Dad and I prayed to God, and I went to the new school by faith. The lady who was in charge of checking the students' boxes went over mine and was at a loss for words. "How are you going to survive in school without all the items you need?" she asked.

"My father is going to bring them to me as soon as possible. We did not have enough money, and I do not want to lose my chance," I replied.

The lady's gaze was full of compassion. Turning to my father she said, "Please make sure that you do not take more than two weeks. You have come from so far away. I do not want to send you back with your daughter."

"Thank you very much," said Father.

Normally I would have been sent back home to get everything together before being enrolled. In this way, many young people from poor families lost their chance for further education, especially in the best schools. By the time the poor child finished collecting the items, the chance would be given to another child on the waiting list. Usually those who did not receive high marks

God Makes a Way

on their exams but had money ready to pay were admitted. By God's grace, this did not happen to me. God answered my prayers.

On completing the advanced level of education course (A level), the board of governors of Mutitu SDA Secondary School, my former secondary school, employed me to teach English and literature in English.

At that point, I became a secondary school teacher. My mother's dream had come true. I had worked hard in school so that I could become a teacher of English and literature in English. But I knew God had enabled me to achieve the success. This achievement made my mother so happy that she fell in love with the Adventist system of education. The academic achievement earned me my freedom to keep the Sabbath without interference from any family member. Around the same time, my father retired with no benefits and no savings whatsoever, so I became the sole breadwinner for the family. I enrolled my two sisters in the same Adventist secondary school I had attended, and I had the privilege of teaching them. They too became Sabbathkeepers. Later more family members became Adventist church members, mostly through attending Adventist schools.

However, the feeling of contentment did not last long. Soon I faced a big challenge: I needed to go to college for further training. Due to the huge financial responsibilities I had for my family, I could not save money to go back to school. Yet, I wanted to secure my career quickly so that I could get married and raise a family. Every young lady was supposed to get married. Throughout our lives we were trained and socialized for marriage. By then, almost all the young people my age were married, and my mother and my grandmother were starting to become concerned to the point of suggesting potential husbands for me.

According to my parents, I needed to marry a Christian young man whose father had a big piece of land and many cows. As for me, a Seventh-day Adventist with some college education was the ideal man if I loved him and trusted his love for me. There was none in my village or in the neighboring villages. However, the wrong men could never leave me alone. Some even attempted to marry me by force, failure to which they threatened to kill me.

I asked God to make a way for me to go to college and give me the kind of a man I desired for a husband. Then, I waited.

Chapter 4

God Gave Me the Desires of My Heart

A colleague at Mutitu SDA Secondary School shared Romans 8:28 with me: "And we know that all things work together for good to them that love God, to them who are the called according to his purpose." I just looked at him and sighed. I thought he did not understand how desperate my situation was. In appreciation for his concern, I nodded my head and wished him and his wife a good night before slowly walking to my quiet house. As I walked from the teachers' quarters toward the girls' dorms up the hill and to the other teachers' houses near the road where I lived, I wondered what good could come out of my disappointing and frustrating situation.

By this time, I had been teaching at this Adventist secondary school for three years. All this time, I was teaching as an untrained teacher, and I could not be paid a salary as good as that of teachers who had diplomas or degrees in education. Therefore, I so much wanted to get a degree in education. However, I did not have money to pay for my education at a university. As a result, I sought admission to the government's diploma colleges that charged very little money due to the government's subsidy.

To be admitted to the colleges, one had to sit for an interview, and the competition was very stiff because there were very few colleges and thousands of young teachers to be trained. I applied every year for three years, and I was always invited for interviews, but for the three long years, I was never accepted. To make matters worse, my best friend, Josephine, who was like my twin sister, was accepted on her third try.

Josephine and I had gone to school together from form two to form six. We went to the same secondary school and the same high school. We were converted to the Adventist faith around the same time, and we were baptized together by the same pastor. After form six, we were both employed to teach English and literature in English at Mutitu SDA School. We also lived in the same house as teachers. This is the same friend who had given me a pair of sheets and a towel when I reported to school without enough stuff to use. So long as we were together, we encouraged each other and kept waiting for the time when we would be accepted to college.

When Josephine was at last called to join the college and I was left out, my world seemed to have come to an end. For several months, I could not function properly. I cried for many days. I became very disappointed, frustrated, and stressed. I grew so thin that my clothes did not fit me anymore. I was very tired of teaching as an untrained teacher. By this time, I was thinking of getting married, but I feared getting married before I was trained as a teacher. Many times married women did not get a chance to go to school. There were extremely few men who would allow their wives to go to school no matter what. In fact, many men were known to deny their wives permission to work away from the home no matter how much education the woman had.

For that reason, I wanted to get done with my schooling before getting married so that I could strike a perfect balance between productive and reproductive duties as a woman. I so badly wanted to go to college. *Why is it taking forever for me to be accepted? Why was I left out as Josephine was admitted? We had similar qualifications, and we have been waiting for three years together. How much longer am I going to wait before I get admitted to the diploma college?* I asked myself these endless questions.

By this time, I had met a young man who worked in Nairobi. He was a Christian and a Sabbathkeeper. After a few months as my boyfriend, he proposed to me, and I accepted. However, after some time, I observed some behaviors that I did not want to deal with in my marriage. But before I could break the relationship, the young man sent his father to my father with goats for the dowry. Unfortunately, he did this without consulting me. I was teaching far away from home, and I could not know these things unless somebody from home told me. A month or so later, my mother came to visit me at Mutitu and told me what my boyfriend and his family had done. My parents knew that we were courting; they accepted the dowry.

"Just take care of the goats, but don't touch them yet," I told my mother.

"Why?" she asked.

"Nobody told me anything about paying a dowry for me, and I need to understand what's happening."

"Whatever the case, the goats are ours now. You are soon getting married, aren't you?"

"I don't know," I said.

"Culture has it that if you don't marry the man who has paid a dowry for you, the dowry will stay at your father's home. The man who does marry you finally will pay back the dowry to the first man," Mother explained.

"How did I get into this mess? Why did my boyfriend pay a dowry without consulting me?" I asked her.

"We thought the two of you had agreed," said Mother.

At this point, I changed the topic because to Mom it did not matter so much whether I was consulted or not. After all, in the olden days, during the times of my grandmother and my mother, parents arranged the marriages of their children. The children, especially the girl, was just informed that a certain family had paid a dowry for her and that she would get married whenever the husband-to-be deemed it fit. But as for me, nobody was going to drag me into a marriage that I felt uncomfortable about no matter what.

After Mother went back home to Makueni, I went to Nairobi the following weekend to see my boyfriend and obtain an explanation.

"I want us to get married in December. That's why I paid the dowry, and I have set up a committee to organize our wedding," he told me.

I heard the words and felt like I was dreaming. I looked at him in disbelief. *This is one of the things I sensed when I decided to break the engagement. My opinions are not important. I have to be instructed on everything, even on things that affect me so directly.*

"Why didn't you consult me before doing all this?" I asked him.

"I was going to tell you soon so that you could start preparing yourself," he said.

"I'm not ready for marriage now," I said.

"You know the whole wedding is my responsibility. You don't need to do anything. I will buy the wedding dress for you and anything else that you need," he told me.

Of course I knew, besides paying a dowry for the bride, culture had it that the whole wedding was the man's responsibility. All a bride had to do was to pick out the wedding dress and make sure that her bridesmaids were dressed the way she wanted; however, each bridesmaid paid for her own dress for the wedding.

"Psychologically, I am not ready. I need time," I told him.

"How much time do you need?" he asked.

"One year."

"OK, I will give you one year,"

I did not see the need to keep arguing about why my boyfriend had paid a dowry and started the wedding preparation without consulting me. That then was spilled water. In any case, the old culture had it that once a man had paid a dowry for a girl, he did not need her consent to marry her or to decide when to do it. Often, the man just watched the girl as she went to the river to fetch water or as she went to get firewood in the forest and with the help of his friends carried her away to his home. Then, the man's family would send somebody to report to the girl's parents that the girl had gotten married. However, I did not want to deal with that kind of an attitude in my husband. And I knew there was almost nothing I could do to change him at his age.

All the same, I was very careful with this conversation. I did not want to make him suspicious of my plans or tell him to his face that I wanted to end our relationship. I knew it was not safe for me to do that in his house. I wanted to tell him when he came to visit me at my place of work or tell him in writing. Soon an opportunity offered itself, and I told him that I was not going to marry him and that he was free to find another woman to marry.

He could not take it. He had to marry me no matter what. But I knew I would not marry him because I did not see myself happily married to him. Anyway, I had told him my stand, and I was done with the engagement.

I continued praying to God to give me the kind of a man I desired for a husband. Nonetheless, there were so many other young men seeking my hand in marriage. Some were Christians and Sabbathkeepers, but others were not. I knew I did not want to marry any of them because in them I did not see what I wanted in my husband.

I wanted a man who could love me in the deepest sense of the word, and one who would treat me with respect as his life partner. I had to love him too. This had to be a man I could easily submit to and one I would willingly support to achieve his goals in life. And he too had to be willing to do the same for me. But I did not want a man who had a prescription for what I would do throughout my life whether I liked it or not. In addition, this man had to have some college education. I thought this would enhance our communication and understanding, in addition to providing financial security for the family.

However, before looking for these qualities, I wanted a serious Christian and a Seventh-day Adventist too. After all the trouble and pain I went through before I got permission to keep the Sabbath, I was not going to lose that freedom by marrying a non-Sabbathkeeper. Usually, a woman had to go to her husband's church, and even when the husband did not go to any church, he had to permit the wife to go to a certain church.

I knew it would be easier for me to submit to a loving, caring, and respectful husband and let him have his place as the head of the family than if he was demeaning and insensitive to my needs.

Several months after Josephine had gone to college, a young man by the name David came to teach in the same school I was at. David was an Adventist and the son of Pastor Nahashon Itumo, an Adventist pastor from Mbooni. After a few weeks of teaching together at Mutitu SDA Secondary School, we became friends. Then one day he told me he wanted to marry me. I thought he was teasing me, but he seriously proposed to me.

He seemed to have most of the qualities I wanted in my husband, though he told me that he did not have a house and that we would be living in a cave. That sounded very interesting to me. No other man had ever been so open with me about his poverty. I, however, knew that he was not as poor as he wanted me to believe. After praying and searching myself, I accepted his proposal. David had recently graduated from the university with a degree in business administration. He and his family did not have a big farm or many cows, but they had Jesus and enough of everything else they needed, cows and land included.

David proposed that we should get married quickly. I told him I had to go to college first, but he promised to take me to college after we got married. I trusted him. A few months later we went to visit my parents so they could meet him. As culture had it, my father could not discuss anything with David alone. His parents had to be there. A few weeks later, David and his parents went to see my parents to request that they give me to David for marriage. My parents accepted, and we soon started formal marriage negotiations.

Unfortunately, my former boyfriend heard about it and decided that nobody was going to marry me except himself. He started issuing death threats to both David and I. All the same, David's parents sent elders to take back the dowry he had paid for me. Before the wedding, David, with the help of his parents and other relatives, had to pay a dowry and cook for my relatives, neighbors, and friends, who totaled more than a hundred people. All negotiations and other functions went seamlessly. The wedding preparations went well too. Although we had many bridesmaids and groomsmen, they were well organized. Each paid for his or her wedding clothes in time. The time for the wedding came at last. However, there was drama on the wedding day!

Chapter 5

A Wedding or Eloping at Night?

As was the practice, the night before the wedding day, the bridegroom and his parents and a few relatives would go to the bride's home and spend the night there. The bride's parents and relatives would cook for the visitors and hold talks to guide the young people on what was expected of each one of them after the wedding and throughout their lives together. On the wedding day, the whole group would proceed to the church where the wedding ceremony was to take place. David and I made similar plans. My relatives, neighbors, and friends gathered at my father's home the day before the wedding and cooked for David and his relatives who were to arrive at my home at 8:00 p.m. the night before the wedding day.

Unfortunately, my relatives cooked and waited for David and his family from 8:00 p.m. to 1:00 p.m. the day of the wedding. There were no telephones or cell phones to call and find out whether David may have changed his mind, as some of my relatives feared might have happened.

"When did you last see your husband-to-be?" one of my relatives asked me.

"A week ago, before I left school," I said.

"Did you part peacefully?" she asked.

"Yes, we agreed that I should take one week off to come home and stay with my mother before the wedding day. His people and he had completed plans about how they would come here the night before the wedding," I replied. She kept quiet after this, but I could tell from the look on her face that she had more questions.

The wedding was to start at 10:00 a.m., and it was to take place in Mbooni, at least a four-hour drive through the forest's rough roads. It was already 10:00 a.m. Yet, nobody knew what had become of David and his family. Then, at 1:00 p.m. we heard some noise of a moving vehicle from afar. As the noise approached, most people stood outside to see who it was. David and his family had arrived. By the time the minibus stopped in front of my mother's hut, my relatives had surrounded the vehicle to welcome the visitors and to find out what had happened.

"Last evening, at around 8:00 p.m., we got stuck in a river," one of David's uncles said.

"Which route did you come by?" asked my father.

"We came through Itumbule. David wanted us to come through Makongo, but some of our people thought Itumbule was shorter, and we were already late. We got stuck in a river there which does not have a bridge. Water was running through. The driver could not see where there was sand and where there was mud. We stayed there for fifteen hours. At 11:00 a.m. a tractor passed by and it pulled us out of the river," explained David's uncle.

"It is terribly late. What shall we do, *Syitawa* (in-law)?" David's father asked my father.

"I think we should leave for church immediately. We have had many sittings and lengthy talks in the past. Let the children go get married. We will hold more talks later," suggested my father.

All the people agreed. Quickly, a few ladies came in to the kitchen where I sat listening to the talk.

"Susana, we need to leave for the church now. Where is your suitcase?" one asked.

I stood up and led them to my bedroom. By then I had built a permanent house for my parents. It consisted of brick and cement walls, and the roof was covered with iron sheets. I had a room there where I slept whenever I came home. All I had to carry from my father's home was a suitcase of my clothes. Everything else I left for my parents. The ladies took my suitcase to the minibus. We left for church a few minutes past 1:00 p.m.

On the way to church, the minibus that carried us stopped three times. The vehicle kept losing power, causing it to stop for about fifteen to twenty minutes. Then it would start again and move pretty well as if nothing had happened. The driver and a few other people on board checked the vehicle, but they could not detect any problem. The minibus was not heating up or anything. This was too strange for anybody to explain.

At long last, we arrived at the church a few minutes before 6:00 p.m. To our surprise, the church and the whole compound was full of relatives, friends, colleagues, and church members from far and near who had waited for us the whole day. Among the people who had waited was Pastor Joseph Kyale, the then-president of the East African Union, who officiated our wedding. Mrs. Jemimah Kyale was there, too.

As soon as the minibus stopped in front of the church, people shouted praises to God. Others burst out in song. In the midst of all these, as soon as I stepped out of the vehicle, Mrs. Kyale came straight to me.

"Susana, I'm so glad you made it. This is your day. Please come with me and change into your wedding dress. We will start the wedding as soon as you are ready," she told me.

"My wedding dress is in my suitcase which is on the minibus," I replied.

"Can I get somebody to carry the bride's suitcase for me?" Mrs. Kyale requested.

"I will," said one of the young men standing by.

"Please keep it outside that door," Mrs. Kyale said, pointing to a closed door on the side of the church.

"Please come with me, Susana," she told me.

Mrs. Kyale opened the closed door as she pulled in my suitcase and repeated, "We will start the wedding as soon as you are ready."

She went out and left me to get dressed. From my home to the church I had traveled in a short-sleeved purple and cream kitenge, African attire which I had bought for that purpose. The slightly loose top with a fitting long wrap skirt flattered my tall, slender figure. I quickly changed into my white, long-sleeved wedding dress and slightly high-heeled white shoes. After a few minutes, Mrs. Kyale and my maid of honor came in to help fix my crown and the long net behind my dress. David, too, changed into his black suit, white shirt, black bowtie, and black shoes. Unfortunately, our parents did not change into their new clothes we had bought for the wedding. They stayed in the same clothes they had traveled in. People only seemed to care that David and I got married.

Nobody cared about dressing up anymore.

A few minutes to 6:00 p.m. as many people as the church could accommodate were seated. Those who could not find space inside the church stayed outside and watched through the windows. Our bridesmaids and groomsmen dressed for the occasion—the bridesmaids wore white skirt suits with blue ribbons and white shoes, while the groomsmen dressed in black suits, white shirts, black bowties, and black shoes.

The bridesmaids and groomsmen were paired together and marched in to music from a cassette player that sounded as if it was performing its best that day. The Swahili song said, "*Mwanadamu anaharusi tatu za maisha. Katika hizo tatu ni moja tu hufurahi. Shangilia, Shangilia, Shangilia.*" (A human being has three great occasions in his or her life: birth, wedding, and burial. Of those three occasions, it's only during wedding time when a person celebrates because his or her eyes can see. So, celebrate, celebrate, celebrate.)

This song revitalized the whole church compound. People were thrown into a celebrating mood. We marched to our reserved seats in the church. Although it was late, the bridesmaids and groomsmen still marched as they had practiced: one step forward, a half step backward, then another long step forward.

However, as soon as we finished marching and settled down in church, the sun set completely, and darkness filled the church. We could not see properly.

"Please, light lamps and place them at strategic places in here so we can all see," the master of ceremony requested of the young men in the church. As the lamps were being lighted, various thoughts rushed through my mind: *I refused to elope at night so as to do a wedding and get married in broad daylight. Why did my wedding have to be at night?* However, as much as I felt disappointed about getting married at night, I could not dare suggest that we postpone the wedding. And the main reason was that we spent almost all the money that we had to prepare for that day.

Secondly, I wanted to get married so that my former boyfriend would stop threatening and harassing David and me. I did not share my feelings with anybody. To the rest of the world, I was just calm and quiet as always, but deep inside my heart I was asking God why. I do not know where the pressure lamps and lanterns came from. All I saw were lamps placed at various places in the church. Then there was enough light for us to do whatever we needed to do.

"Those who have cars outside, please switch on the headlamps so that those who are outside can see," the master of ceremony requested again. Soon the whole church compound was full of light. As soon as we finished exchanging vows and signing our marriage certificate, and after listening to a few remarks from Pastor Kyale, we left the church. The reception was outside in the church compound. During this time I smiled broadly for the first time in twenty-four hours. We cut our wedding cake. David cut a fist-size piece of cake and tried to feed me. I knew that even if I wanted to imitate a python, I could not open my mouth wide enough to accommodate the piece. I gave him an eloquent look. For a few seconds, he just gave me a smile and held out the cake. The whole crowd laughed. Then he put down the big piece and gave me one I could comfortably eat.

After the cake eating session, we received presents that many people had carried for us. These ranged from money, plates, cups, glasses, blankets, towels, goats, tables, etc. At around 11:00 p.m. the long day came to a close. We carried our presents and went home. However, for weeks, months, and years I kept asking myself, *Why did my wedding have to be at night?*

Just the same, two days after the wedding, we went on our honeymoon to the coast to swim in the Indian Ocean. By the time we went back to Mutitu SDA School where we taught, my disappointment had eased. Nevertheless, whenever I looked at the wedding pictures and saw pressure lamps and lanterns all over the church, I remembered I had been married at night. Why? *This is one question I plan to ask God when I go to heaven.*

Ten months after our wedding I enrolled at the University of Eastern Africa, Baraton, the Adventist University in Kenya. By then, I was four months pregnant. Although we did not earn much money, God provided in many ways. To start with, David had some dollars he had earned from his canvassing in Sweden. He paid for me to start school.

Then, in a shopping center next to the university, I started a retail shop, which did very well. I sold secondhand clothes, *kiodos* (baskets), and most other items found in retail shops. I also rented a five-acre farm and planted maize, which I sold. Both the farming and the shop provided enough money for food, rent, and money to pay a maid to look after our little son so that I could attend class. By this time, David had become an accountant in the East African Union. Although he did not earn much money, God blessed us, and he was able to pay for my tuition until I finished my course.

Looking back at all the work I did as a mother, a student, a businesswoman, and a farmer, while maintaining a good GPA, I know for sure God gave me grace, because everything I touched prospered. In addition, I did all this work in a strange land where I had no relatives or family to support me, apart from my little boy, Wisdom. The University of Eastern Africa, Baraton, was approximately 500 miles away from Nairobi where my husband was working. He visited me at least twice every month. God gave me courage and strength to accomplish all I needed.

Since I had always wanted a university degree, I felt so fulfilled when I obtained it. I wondered why I had been so frustrated and stressed for not getting admitted to the diploma colleges. Now I understood why God had not allowed me to go to the diploma college. God knew I did not want a diploma. I wanted a degree, but I thought I could never go to a university because I had no money to pay for my education. But at the right time, God gave me a husband, a son, and the degree I always wanted.

"Our heavenly father has a thousand ways to provide for us of which we know nothing" (Ellen G. White, *The Ministry of Healing*, p. 481). I wish I had not allowed myself to get as frustrated as I had. Now I understand that just because I am limited in my options, it does not mean I have no way out. I learned that God is not limited as I am. *When will I ever finish college, get a job, get married, and have children?* I always wondered. I did not realize that with God much of all that would be accomplished in one year. In fact, four years later, as I graduated from the university, I was four months pregnant, expecting our daughter, Lulu.

Today, I thank God that He gave me exactly what I sincerely desired, but not what I thought I could only achieve. All the time I cried as I anxiously waited to be admitted to the diploma college, I did not know that God kept me waiting a little longer only to give me the best and the true desires of my heart.

From this experience I understood the exact meaning of the verse, "And we know that all things work together for good to them that love God, to them who are the called according to his purpose" (Rom. 8:28).

Chapter 6

Mystery Solved

Seven years after our wedding, David met a man who introduced himself as a broker who sold plots, pieces of land, in the city of Nairobi in addition to being a police reservist. The man convinced David that he could get for him a good plot in the city at a reasonable price. David told the broker to let him know when he got a good plot. Then one day, the broker came to our house to discuss with David a plot he had found. Immediately, David introduced the man to me. The man told me, "I know your name is Susana, and you are related to Richard. Before you met David, you were engaged to another man who paid a dowry for you."

"Oh my goodness! How do you know all that? I don't know you!"

"I know you don't know me. David, too, doesn't know that I knew him before we started talking," he said.

"Who are you, and how do you know us?" I asked him.

"I knew both of you even before you got married to each other. Your wedding was in April 1988. You were supposed to die on your wedding day. I, together with some other men, traveled in a private car to Wambuli SDA Church where you wedded. My friends and I kept patrolling the church. We were on a mission to kill both of you. However, you were so delayed that we thought you were not coming at all. We thought you had cancelled the wedding, and we left. Later, we learned that you are related to Richard. Then we called off our mission," he explained.

"Ha! Why did you want to kill us?" I asked.

"You don't want to know the details," he said.

"Do you still want to kill us?" David asked.

"If I still wanted to kill you, I would not be seen with you," he responded.

I looked at the stocky man clad in a grey suit, white shirt, and a tie to match with his almost navy blue face and wondered whether I was looking at a human being or some sort of an alien. Even the Samaritan woman may not have been that shocked by Jesus.

"How did you know that I am related to Richard?" I asked him. The man just smiled coldly and showed me his expressionless face.

Richard is my mother's first cousin, but he lived in a different district far from my home. It was only very close family members from my mother's side who knew that Richard was my relative. *How did this man find out all this information? It must be true that he was out to kill us.* I was shocked by the man's nerve. *How can he come to our house to tell us how he was out to kill us on our wedding day?*

Then I remembered, a few days after our wedding, one of David's aunts told us that there was a white car that patrolled the church area the whole day. The car did not enter the church compound but kept racing through all the routes leading to the church, but it kept turning back at the gate. The car disappeared when it looked like it was too late for the wedding to take place. I did not know how to behave toward this man because he did not sound converted since the time he had wanted to kill us. The only reason why he did not kill us was because I was Richard's niece.

I have never known why my being related to Richard prevented these men from killing us. But deep down in my heart, I know God protected us. After all, the man and his friends could have killed us on our wedding day, because by then they had not known that I was Richard's niece, and that was the day they were looking for David and me to kill us. But God kept the murderers away from us by keeping us away from the church area by all means.

After the confession, my disappointment about my wasted wedding day vanished. All this time, I could not understand why I had labored so much to plan a wedding instead of eloping at night, only to have my wedding from around six in the evening to around eleven at night. It was during this time that I was able to see the purpose of all the strange things that had happened the day before our wedding and during our special day. I always wondered how it happened that for a whole fifteen hours no vehicle went through the route where David and his relatives were stuck. Although it was during the rainy season and the route was known to be bad, some vehicles like tractors went through.

In addition, as we traveled to Mbooni on the day of the wedding, we witnessed very strange things. Besides the minibus stopping a few times and failing to move for no apparent reason, there was one big river that we had had to cross near the church. Immediately after crossing the river, it filled with water. Apparently, it had rained on the mountains and water had come down. This water almost swept our car down the river. Immediately we went across, everybody held his or her breath. I kept asking myself, *What is all this? Where is God when my wedding is so messed up?* After the strange man narrated to us their failed operation plan, I realized that God had used all the delaying techniques so that we would not meet the killers. I'm still amazed by this miraculous salvation that God organized and executed for David and me on our wedding day.

Then, after thinking for some time about the strange man who had enough nerve to confess to us that he and his friends had wanted to kill us, I thought God had allowed the man to come and confess so that I would understand why our wedding had to take place at night. I thought God was so kind to lift the burden from my heart because until my death, I would never have been consoled by anything about my wasted wedding day. Wasting the day to save David's life and mine made perfect sense.

Yes, "All things work together for good to them that love God, to them who are the called according to his purpose."

Chapter 7

Miracle Deliverance

After I graduated from the University of Eastern Africa, Baraton, in June 1993, I moved from Eldoret to Nairobi to join David. It was there that I joined New Life SDA Church in Nairobi where David was worshipping. Although the city hall where we worshipped was a big place, the church had grown so much that almost a quarter of the church members sat outside as they listened to the sermons.

Consequently, the church was divided into five churches. The new churches were opened in different parts of Nairobi, and all the people in the main church were divided according to where they lived and were placed into those five churches. David and I were sent to New Life SDA Church, Riruta Satellite. There were about forty grown-ups when we first started the new church at Riruta. In spite of the fact that we worshipped in one of the classrooms at Ndurarua Primary School, Nairobi, it was a blessing to have a smaller church. Almost all of us had responsibilities in the church.

I became the women's ministry leader and a choir member. David, too, sang in the choir, and he also taught the Pathfinders. Everybody seemed to have a revival since we were few enough to greet each other and share our joys and our concern.

The church was warm and friendly—Sabbaths were a total blessing. We sang and gave testimonies, and every Sabbath the church congregation prayed for two families in the church. The two families would stand in front of the church and the pastor, whenever he was available, and church elders would surround the families and lead the church to pray for the two families. Whenever my family got this chance, it was a very peaceful and reassuring experience.

Soon we started prayer cells. Several people were grouped together to form the prayer cells, depending on how close they lived to each other. These prayer cells met on Friday evenings to welcome the Sabbath, at which time the members would pray together and give testimonies. The Holy Spirit seemed to be closer to us then than at any other time in my life. Personally, I received any petition I gave to God in prayer through my prayer cell. It felt very comforting to belong to such a church.

One Friday evening David and I went to welcome the Sabbath in one of our prayer cell member's home. By the time we finished our Bible study, testimonies, and prayer, it was 10:00 p.m. We did not have a car; we used public transport, riding the bus to our apartment. On alighting from the bus, we took the estate road to our house. There were no streetlights, and the neighborhood seemed quiet. Apart from David and I, no other people were walking on the road at that time. However, after walking for about three minutes, at which time we were only about one hundred meters from our apartment, we saw a group of men coming from the opposite direction. Although it was dark, I sensed that they were thugs.

At once I shared my thought with David. "Dave, those are thugs."

He did not say anything. "Dave, those are thugs," I repeated.

"Please be calm and keep walking," David told me.

We could not turn back because by the time we saw them, they were very close to us. In my panic, I just prayed, "God help us."

There was no time for a long prayer. The men were in two pairs about ten steps apart. The first two came straight to us and blocked our way; their short axes were raised high. As we stood still, they came close and looked at our faces. To our surprise, they quickly gave way as each one moved to the side of the road, to the left and to the right, leaving us in the middle. We resumed walking.

The next pair came straight to us and blocked our way by standing in front of us with their swords drawn, ready to attack, and at the same time demanding money. We neither said a word nor did we give them any money. Then they came close and looked at us. To our surprise, they behaved just like the first two thugs. With our path clear, we walked quickly to the house.

God Makes a Way

By the time we entered the apartment, we were overjoyed because of what we had seen. We had just witnessed a miracle! This part of Nairobi borders the Kawangware slums, which is known for hardcore criminals. Usually, thugs badly harm their victims, if they leave them alive at all. We wondered why they had not even taken our watches or frisked us for money.

On reaching our house, we worshipped and praised God for performing this miracle for us. Although I knew God had saved us, I kept wondering what it was that had made the thugs to look at our faces and then move away as if they were frightened by something.

Moreover, our next-door neighbor and a church member also experienced the same miraculous deliverance that we had when he and his sister were car jacked. The thugs had taken them far outside the city to a forest, but all they did was rob our neighbor of the little money he had in his pocket. Many times, when thugs take people outside the city to a forest, they torture and kill them. Another surprising thing was that the thugs abandoned our neighbor's car near his home without vandalizing it.

We lived in this compound for more than ten years. This was a building with four apartments. Most of the time the apartments were occupied by church members, because when somebody moved out, we told a friend or somebody we knew from college or church, so they could move in.

We had other buildings on the left and on the right. What was surprising was that several times robbers broke into those neighboring buildings. The owners would scream as the robbers continued hitting the doors with stone blocks until they broke down. These were very scary experiences, both for us and our neighbors. Yet, for the more than ten years we lived in these apartments, no thugs ever tried to break into any of our building's apartments. People thought our apartments were strong. But the truth is that "the angel of the LORD encampeth round about them that fear him, and delivereth them" (Ps. 34:7).

The following day at church we told the church members about our miraculous deliverance. They praised God for His tender care and faithfulness. "Behold, the eye of the LORD is upon them that fear him, upon them that hope in his mercy; To deliver their soul from death, and keep them alive in famine" (Ps. 33:18, 19). "Thou art my hiding place; thou shalt preserve me from trouble; thou shalt compass me with songs of deliverance" (Ps. 32:7).

Chapter 8

Peace Beyond Understanding

"Many are the afflictions of the righteous: but the LORD delivereth him out of them all" (Ps. 34:19).

In December 1999 I had finished one year and one quarter at the University of East African, Baraton, pursuing a master's degree in education. David was still working in Nairobi. It was during this time when my father-in-law, Pastor Nahashon Itumo, fell sick and was admitted to a hospital in Nairobi. After two weeks, he passed away, and for a moment, I thought the world had come to an end. I could not imagine our family without my father-in-law. He was always so supportive and encouraging to all of us. He always told us to endure trials and hardships in life. He likened life to a long rope with different colors.

"The rope keeps turning, showing people different colors at different times in their lives. Sometimes it shows green, which means that things are working out well for that person at that time. But whenever it shows red that means that person is going through a hard time. Maybe the person is sick; maybe he is experiencing financial difficulties or any other problem in life. However, that person should persevere and endure the hardship, knowing that soon the red will pass and a better color will show up, which means things will get better. And those who trust in the Lord should be more encouraged because they know that God is able to change situations. In addition, during the hard times, God is always with us, providing sufficient grace to see us through whatever we must experience in life," he always told us.

Many times my father-in-law encouraged us to work hard and always be ready to sacrifice convenience or comfort to achieve a desired goal in life. He kept reminding us how the Mau Mau, the men who fought for Kenya's independence, chose to go to the forest and live in caves for many years in an effort to gain freedom for the country. He always told us to imagine leaving the comfort of home to go live in a cave without freedom to come out for treatment if one was sick or to get food without risking to be shot dead on sight. He mostly told us this story to encourage us, his children, to get an education and fight poverty. And he would remind us that Jesus left real comfort in heaven to come and die for us. "Therefore, your ultimate goal in life should be to prepare yourself for the coming of Jesus Christ and to help others to do the same," he would tell us.

Before my father-in-law passed away, I traveled from Baraton to Nairobi to see him. His throat had been operated on, and he was very swollen. I told him, "Father, you will be well."

"Muthembwa, let the will of God be done," he told me. (To respect me, he called me by my grandfather's name. That's our culture).

After a few days, he passed away. When I heard about it, I knew he had surrendered his will into the hands of our wise, loving God. But I thought of David who had been nursing him in the hospital. *How is he going to handle my mother-in-law?* I wondered. The day his father passed away, my mother-in-law did not go to the hospital. David had left her at his house in Nairobi. As soon as his father passed away, David's uncle, Professor Mutinga, arrived at the hospital. This is my mother-in-law's big brother. He then called my mother-in-law and informed her about the death of her husband. This would have been very hard for David to do, but God provided help and support just when David desperately needed it.

We buried my father-in-law on December 14, 1999. Then we stayed home in the village with my mother-in-law for the remaining days of December. Then we went back to Nairobi immediately after the New Year holiday. Two days later, somebody knocked on our gate. It was a colleague of David's. He brought David a letter of suspension from work. The reasons did not make sense to us. All the same, he was suspended without pay until further notice.

This was a very trying time for us because I was a graduate student at the university. In addition, we lived in the city in a rented house. We had no idea how to raise money for rent. Also, our young children were in a private school in the city. How would we pay their school and transportation fees?

Furthermore, by this time, I was eight months pregnant with our third baby.

I was glad that I was in Nairobi with David when the suspension letter came. Unfortunately, a week after this suspension, our son became sick and had to have an emergency operation. By God's grace the operation was successful. And with all these troubles, I was supposed to be collecting data from The Kenya Institute of Education, Nairobi. I was supposed to interview the Literature Curriculum Planners and find out what criteria they used to choose literature books for Kenyan secondary schools. I then had to analyze five literature set books, a sample of the literature set books that had been used in Kenyan secondary schools for the previous five years to see if what the curriculum planners said was reflected in those books. God gave me the strength and peace I needed to do all that. I finished collecting data, analyzed it, and wrote down my findings. Then I decided to go back to Eldoret, to the university, to consult with my supervisors.

I was due to deliver our baby in four weeks. Therefore, I decided to go to the university so that after a week of discussions with my professors I could return to Nairobi to continue analyzing my data as I waited to deliver our baby. But before I left for the university, I decided to go to the hospital for a checkup and consultation with my doctor to find out whether it was safe to travel for more than 300 kilometers by road. The doctor examined me and seemed to be very shocked.

"What's wrong?" I asked her.

"Your baby is very big," she told me.

"Does that mean I will go for a cesarean section?" I asked.

"Probably," she said.

"Can I safely travel to Baraton?" I inquired.

"Sure. You can go," she said.

The following day, David and I left for the University of Eastern Africa, Baraton. Now that David was suspended from work, he could take me to the college because I feared to travel alone for such a long distance at this stage of my pregnancy. We arrived in the evening. I was very tired, but I rested and in the morning I felt strong enough to see my supervisors. However, by 1:00 p.m. I noticed that I had not felt the movement of my baby since the previous night, so I went to the university clinic. The doctor who examined me told me that she could not hear any movement. She advised me to go to the town of Eldoret for an ultrasound.

After the ultrasound, I asked the radiologist, "Is it a boy or a girl?"

He ignored my question and asked me, "When did you last feel any movement of your baby?"

"I think the day before yesterday," I said.

"He is dead," he told me.

"Dead? Why?" I was shocked.

"Do you have anybody with you?" the radiologist asked.

"Yes, I have my husband and my sister-in-law in the waiting room," I answered.

"Tell your husband to take you to Eldoret Memorial Hospital immediately."

Upon reaching the hospital, the doctor who examined me told David and me that my condition was very serious. He told me to make up my mind to hold on to life. Then David prayed to God to sustain my life. After the prayer, he started pleading with me. "Susan, please live for the children and me. Please don't give up on life."

"Continue praying for me," I told him.

I spent more than twenty-four hours in the hospital with the doctor trying in vain to induce labor. Nothing is as difficult and painful as delivering an oversized dead fetus. All the same, David's words for me to hold onto life rang in my mind throughout the ordeal. I literally called on Jesus to save me even when it felt like I had no chance of survival.

After sixteen hours of forced labor, the baby finally came out—a big baby boy. The doctor said he had been dead for at least three days. Since that day, my life was never the same again. I thought I would die from the pain I felt in my heart. I slept and thought I would not wake up. *Why did my baby die?*

The doctor had told me I had gestational diabetes. I had started going to the hospital for checkups after the first month of pregnancy. One time I collapsed in the city of Nairobi. When I gained strength, I went straight to one of the best hospitals in the city. The lab technician said I had signs of diabetes. The doctor asked me to go back the following day to get my fasting blood sugar checked. Afterwards, the doctor told me I didn't have diabetes. And now my baby was dead from gestational diabetes after going to the clinic every month for eight months. *Why?*

After one week in the hospital, I went back to the college. I was too sick to travel to Nairobi. But I was a tutor at the university, and I had been given an apartment on the campus. Teachers and students came to see me there, but I was too sad to be comforted. Then one day a couple, Mr. and Mrs. Mbaya, came to see me. As we talked I told them I was wondering where God was when my baby died. "I'm alive just because God did not allow death. I know I should be dead now. Very few women survive such an ordeal," I said.

Mr. Mbaya asked me, "Suppose somebody told you that the baby would live but that he would never talk, never sit on his own, never feed himself, or never take himself to the bathroom for the rest of his life, would you still choose to have him?

"I don't know," I said.

"You have heard people ask, 'Where was God when His Son was whipped and nailed on the cross until He died, and I want to ask you the same question because you are wondering where He was when your son died," Mr. Mbaya told me.

"God watched His Son die to save the world. What did my son die for?" I asked.

"What did the doctors tell you?" he asked.

"Gestational diabetes was the problem. But why didn't the doctors detect it early enough to save my baby? I have been going to the hospital for checkups for eight months?" I said.

"These are some of the things we will never understand in this world. The best thing to do, though, is to keep trusting in God's love and faithfulness. One day we will understand," Mr. Mbaya explained.

We sang "All the Way My Savoir Leads Me" and "Does Jesus Care?" We then prayed and the couple left. Since that day my sadness started to slowly disappear. In two weeks we went back to Nairobi. Church members came and prayed with us and encouraged us so much.

After a few weeks, we experienced so much peace. Although the loss was still fresh in our minds, though we still mourned the death of my father-in-law and the baby, we were able to experience peace in our lives. In fact, when some of our friends came to see us, they wondered how to start comforting and encouraging us. They did not seem to know what to say about our misfortunes, but we would tell them how God had given us incredible peace. Although David was without pay for eight months, God provided for us. We always had food to eat. The school our children attended did not send them home for school fees. Our landlord never threatened to put us out of the house. By God's grace, all these people were patient with us.

David was called back to work after eight months, and he was paid in arrears for the eight months he had not worked. However, we still did not get any reasonable explanation as to why he had been suspended in the first place. By God's abundant grace, I finished collecting the data for my research, analyzing it, writing my thesis, and presenting it in order to graduate in June 2000. Unfortunately, some of my classmates did not make it. People could not understand how I was able to do all these things after all that I had gone through, but I told them it was all God's doing.

When we were going through these trials, it was very painful. But today we can look back and say, "My brethren, count it all joy when ye fall into divers temptations; Knowing this, that the trying of your faith worketh patience. But let patience have her perfect work, that ye may be perfect and entire, wanting nothing" (James 1:2-4).

Chapter 9

Trusting God Through Threats of Death

"Somebody called the office today and asked to speak to the principal. I asked who the caller was, but he refused to tell me and kept calling every few minutes. After several calls, I told him he could not speak to the principal unless he told me who he was. He hung up and called the deputy principal's cell phone. When the deputy answered, the caller told him, 'Tell the principal we will kill her,'" the school secretary told me.

"Did he say why they want to kill the principal?" I asked.

"No, he did not say anything else," she told me.

"Please call the deputy for me," I told the secretary.

When he got on the phone, he said, "Mrs. Mbaluka, somebody shocked me today. My cell phone rang, and when I looked at it, I saw your cell phone number. But when I answered, a man's voice told me, 'Mr. Deputy Principal, tell the principal we will kill her.'"

"Did you ask him why? I asked.

"I did, but he hung up on me," said the deputy.

I was the principal of Masii SDA Secondary School, so the death threats were directed at me. The previous day I had woken up at 5:00 a.m. to prepare myself to go to Nairobi to purchase laboratory chemicals and textbooks for the school. Since transferring from Kitui Adventist School a year before, I lived at Masii Shopping Center because there was no house for me at the school. There were only two small rooms that were used by the former principal, but he did not live with his family there. I had my teenage children, and they needed their own bedrooms. I needed several rooms for my family.

As a result, the board of governors of the Masii SDA Secondary School rented six rooms for me at Masii Shopping Center. I lived in a plot, a compound with many rooms and many tenants. The toilets and bathrooms were built outside the rooms. This day I needed to be in Nairobi by 9:00 a.m. so that I could finish shopping and travel back to school before 6:00 p.m.

Before I went to the bathroom, I took the documents I needed for this trip and put them in the handbag that I wanted to carry with me. One of these documents was my passport, which I needed to cash the open checks—I operated the school accounts with my passport. I also put my two cell phones, my personal one and the school cell phone, in my bag. In addition, I had some watches that had stopped working. I put them in the bag so that I could take them to Nairobi for new batteries. All these items, together with 2,000 Ksh. (Kenya shillings) I had in cash for the trip and the school checks, totaling 300,000 Ksh. for the school equipment, were in my bag.

I placed the handbag on my bed next to the dress I was going to wear and left for the bathroom to take a bath. Our plot was built to give high security to the tenants. From outside it looked as if a tall stone wall surrounded it. This plot had six rolls or streams of rooms. Every two streams had a back gate and a front gate with very strong metal doors. The doors of the back gates were permanently locked and only the landlord had the keys to them. The front gates, through which every tenant entered, were always locked, and every tenant had a key to the door. Visitors had to knock at the gate for somebody to open it from the inside.

With this sense of security, I did not lock the door to my room because I did not want to carry keys with me to the bathroom. I spent at most fifteen minutes in the bathroom. When I went back to my bedroom, I noticed at once that the handbag, which I had placed on the bed, was missing. By this time, only one of my neighbors was awake. She had woken up after me and went outside the plot without locking the gate. She came back just before I came out of the bathroom. On asking her whether she had seen anybody enter my sitting room, which led to my bedroom, she said yes.

"I took goods to my shop, and immediately after entering the gate from the shop, I saw a tall brown young man coming out of your sitting room. I thought it was your son, Wisdom, but I wondered why he was carrying your handbag," my neighbor told me.

Wisdom was sleeping in his room at the other end of the plot. I did not have all my rooms in a roll. I had two next to the front gate. These two were my sitting room and bedroom. The other four rooms were at the end of the plot: two of these were my children's bedrooms, a kitchen, and a library. Between the first two rooms and the other four were other tenants.

When my neighbor talked of a young man coming out of my sitting room carrying my handbag, my fears were confirmed. Somebody had indeed snuck into my room and had stolen my handbag. I was puzzled. I could not understand how the thief knew that I had gone to the bathroom, and yet when I went, the gate was locked and the other plot members were asleep. *The thief must know me well*, I thought.

In the stolen passport, was my visa to come to America as a missionary teacher. I remembered the five years it had taken me to obtain the visa. Furthermore, replacing a stolen passport in Kenya was a nightmare. I was dazed for some minutes. I prayed, "God of heaven, please help me. I don't know how to deal with this situation."

I decided to tell my family what had happened. First, I went to Wisdom's room and woke him up. The next person to tell was Alice, my sister-in-law, who lived in the same plot, but she entered her rooms through a different gate. When I told her all that was stolen, she immediately started calling my stolen cell phones. To our surprise, the thief answered one of them.

"Please take the money and everything else in the handbag but give us back the documents," Alice pleaded.

"I left the handbag outside your plot. It has all your documents; go get it," said the thief.

We rushed outside and went around the plot, but we did not see anything. After searching for some time, I went to the police station and reported everything. Then I went back to the plot. I found Alice, Wisdom, and our neighbors still searching. By this time I felt dizzy. I could not believe what was happening to me. I sat down in my sitting room and prayed, "God, please give me strength and wisdom to deal with this nightmare. Father, please speak to the thief and instruct him to give my documents back. In Jesus' name, I pray.

Amen." Immediately after I finished praying, a woman knocked on my door but did not enter even though I invited her to do so.

"Madam, I have seen a handbag in the slaughterhouse," she told me.

"What color is it?" I asked.

"It is shiny and black," she said.

The slaughterhouse was about 100 meters from the plot. I knew the handbag this woman described was my stolen bag. Immediately after I heard the news, my strength was renewed. I left quickly with relatives and neighbors following me. Sure enough, it was my handbag. The same woman who had told me its location, pulled it out of a narrow strip where it had been thrown. On opening the bag, the bank checks and my passport were there. When I saw the passport, I did not care about the 2,000 shillings, my two cell phones, or my beautiful watches that the thief had kept.

This was another miracle. Thieves often stole people's passports for business, but a thief took mine and gave it back. He could have easily destroyed the bag and the documents to destroy any evidence of the theft.

Furthermore, I did not even know the woman who came to tell me about my handbag. Her garden bordered the slaughterhouse next to the shopping center, but her home was at the other end of the farm. The bag was hidden from her garden, plus it was too early to be in the garden. I did not even ask her how she had seen the bag. She must have seen people searching her garden and came out to find out what they were doing and then decided to join them in the search. Also, I knew God must have led her to see the bag and bring me the news.

After praying and thanking God for this miracle and thanking all the people who had come out to help me, I left for Nairobi as I had planned. However, instead of going to town to purchase the school supplies, I went straight to Satellite to see my sister, Janiffer. I just wanted to get away from Masii for some time. Although I was happy I got my documents, I was still traumatized. The following day, early in the morning, I went to the city center, cashed the checks, and bought all the goods I needed for school. Then, I went back to school.

However, when the secretary and the deputy told me about the threatening calls from the thief, I panicked. Apparently, the thief had learned that I had reported the case to the police and that the police were looking for him. Hence, the threat to kill me. By the time I arrived at school, it was around six in the evening. Alice and Wisdom had known that the thief was threatening to kill me because he had called Alice's cell phone and had given her the same message. Now that he had my cell phones with all my contacts of friends and relatives, he could call any one of them and relay his threatening message.

I was too scared to go back to the plot. I went to Pastor Benjamin Mutugi's house next to the school compound and asked his wife, Jane, to hide me there. She did. Then she called my son and told him that I would be spending the night at her house. I was glad Lulu had gone back to her boarding school. This would have been too scary for her. Early in the morning the following day, Pastor Mutugi called a taxi to get me and take me to the plot so that I could prepare myself and go back to school.

There was no time to run away or lock myself up in a house to hide from a threatening thief. This was the first week of May 2007. We had just opened school for the second term. Students were coming back to school after the April holidays. Like any other boarding school, the first week of school after a long holiday was packed with responsibilities, making sure that everything, from the dormitories to the classes and the kitchen, was prepared for the 350 students. Furthermore, during this time many parents who did not have school fees ready came to school to talk to the principal to make payment arrangements so that their children could attend school. Also, at the end of this week, I was the one to preach at the school church. And on the following Sabbath, we had invited a choir from Kikima to come and spend the whole day with us at school.

I was preparing to go to the U.S. at the end of the month; I was to leave on May 28, 2007. Before my departure I needed to change bank signatories and hand over responsibilities to my deputy who was to take over the principal's office after I left. Also, I had to sit in school board meetings to update the members on what was happening in school before the deputy principal took over. Furthermore, I had to pack and transport my household goods from the plot to my house in the village. Surely, there was no time to hide.

I, therefore, prayed to God to protect my family and me from any harm and danger. I said, "My Father and my God in heaven, I know that nobody can kill me unless You allow him to. Father, I do not want to die now. And I need to move around freely so that I can do the work that You have given me in this school. Therefore, I surrender my life in Your mighty hands for care and protection." After this prayer, my fear vanished, and I moved around as if nothing had happened.

His Word offered comfort to me through many of the psalms: "Except the LORD keep the city, the watchman waketh but in vain" (Ps. 127:1); "Preserve me, O God: for in thee do I put my trust" (Ps. 16:1); "The LORD is my rock, and my fortress, and my deliverer; my God, my strength, in whom I will trust; my buckler, and the horn of my salvation, and my high tower" (Ps. 18:2).

With trust in my faithful Lord, I worked from sunrise to sunset and did all I needed to do without fear. And God protected me. Until the end of the month when I left for the U.S., I never saw anybody either trailing me or standing in my way. Even the threatening calls ceased after a few days.

Chapter 10

God's Plan Was the Best

I am always excited when the Lord grants the petitions of my prayers. But as I got ready to depart for the U.S, I thanked God for not answering one prayer according to my request.

After thirteen years of marriage, David came to America for further studies. On his departure he hoped that the children and I would follow him within six months. And in case we could not follow him as we hoped, he would work hard and complete his studies in the shortest time possible and come back. The longest we agreed to be separated by distance was two years, the allotted time he needed to complete his master's degree course. But the two years turned into five and a half years.

For all those years, I went to the American Embassy in Kenya looking for visas for our children and me to come to America. The first year I tried to come as a student; the second year the children and I applied to come as my husband's dependents. The rest of the time, I tried to obtain a visa for a few weeks' visit. I was denied visas each time.

Saying I missed my husband is an understatement. Life changed completely for me. I was so lonely; yet, the majority of people never understood what I was going through. In the church people greeted me and treated me as if everything was all right. Among all my relatives, only my mother was constantly bothered by my separation from my husband. I prayed. I cried. I got stressed and frustrated, and then I got used to raising the children alone. Among the questions I asked God were, "God, I prayed for a husband, and You gave me one. I got married because I did not want to live alone. Why did you let my husband go to America if you knew I would not be given the visa to follow him?"

One time, I planned to fast and pray for the visas. I had planned to go to a prayer center in my town where people went and prayed the whole day or even for several days. No food was provided in the center. One could only get water to drink. However, the night before the day of my fasting, I had a dream. In the dream a very powerful voice told me that I was not going to America. I woke up in the morning and still went to the prayer center to cry to God and ask Him why. I went and cried the whole day. Just the same, when I went for the visa the following week, I was denied.

Meanwhile, God blessed me in other ways. By the time my husband left for the U.S., I had already obtained a master's degree in curriculum development and instruction, and I got a job to lecture at a college. God blessed my work at the college. This was a new college in Machakos town, Kenya, and I was employed to organize a curriculum for the Department of Education to train early childhood teachers. In addition, I organized an in-service course to train secondary school teachers in charge of guidance and counseling in various schools, especially in Machakos, Makueni, and Kitui districts. Soon secondary schools started to call me to give lectures on self-esteem, study skills, and examination techniques to students. My department grew and brought in money for the college.

Nonetheless, when the work became too much, the administration required that I start giving lectures on Saturdays. I could not do it because I wanted to keep the Sabbath holy. As a result, when my contract came to an end, the administration did not renew it, and I lost my job.

Although I was no longer employed at the college, I had learned a lot in planning and management. A few months later, I was called to go to one of the Adventist schools in Kenya. This was Kitui SDA School, which had a preschool, elementary, and high school. I went in as the deputy principal of the secondary school section. Six months later, I was promoted to the position of school principal. By this time my son was in a boarding high school. My daughter was in the same school, Kitui, but she chose to be a boarding student so that she could concentrate on her studies. Having been left alone in the house, I was able to concentrate on managing the big school.

It was in this role that I first learned the need to totally depend on God.

First of all, my predecessor adamantly disagreed with the school board of management, and as a result his services were terminated. But instead of leaving, he decided to hand over the conference school to the public to make it a public school. The school was not yet registered in the name of the church—the principal knew he could give it away.

I had never been a principal before, and my predecessor refused to hand things over to me. This was a very big school with around seven hundred students, four hundred of them being boarders. When I was promoted to the principal's office, most documents were in court where my predecessor had sued the school board. It was hard to administer such a big school without records.

In addition, some parents wanted to withdraw their children from the school because of chaos at the time. I had to stand firmly and assure students, parents, and staff that all was well. Up to this day, I marvel at the courage that God gave me at that time. I was verbally and openly threatened. But I prayed, "God, Satan has visited this school in person. Please, God, come to our rescue. Please, Jesus, come in person."

God answered my prayers. He gave me strength and unwavering faith in Him. The Lord enabled me to encourage the students and hold the staff together so that they could help me in reassuring the students and parents. At the same time, I moved very fast to register the school and make the Central Kenya conference the legal owner. God opened doors for me at the Ministry of Education. Within a short time, the school legally belonged to the Central Kenya Conference of the Seventh-day Adventist Church. None of the students were withdrawn from the school at that time.

Within a few weeks, life went back to normal, but every day I prayed, "Lord, God of heaven, please don't ever leave me alone in that office. I cannot last even one day without You." Later that same year, more students were baptized in the school than had ever been baptized before.

However, as I continued working, the pressures kept piling on me. The separation between my husband and I was overwhelming. I prayed, "Lord, please open the way for me to go to America or bring my husband back to Kenya." Unfortunately, as much as I wanted the reunion, misunderstandings developed between David and me. Each one of us got used to making decisions without consulting the other. We became independent of each other and learned to live without each other. We did not understand each other after a few years. We quarreled many times for both real and imaginary reasons. With time each one of us changed because of our experiences and the kind of life we led. We each developed different goals.

At this time, I realized that our separation was the worst thing that had ever happened to our marriage. I started seeing all the consequences of the separation. Besides the differences between us, there were problems from which our children suffered greatly. Immediately after their father left, our daughter became sick. I took her to many doctors, but she did not receive much help. Eventually, I was told she had developed a stomach ulcer at the age of seven. Our son became withdrawn. I realized I had to be strong for our children. Although I was broken inside, I prayed and asked God to give me peace and strength to pull myself together and show the children that all was well. I cried in my bedroom, washed my face, and went out to the children smiling and talking positively. *This separation is not worth anything—not education or money*, I thought.

Just the same, I needed to be strong for both my children and the school where I was an administrator. God gave me courage and peace. The children got better, and they, too, received peace. And by God's grace, they concentrated in school and did very well in their studies. All the same, I continued praying to God to sustain my marriage by His grace. I knew for sure that we had made a big mistake by separating. This was a decision made in total ignorance. But I prayed, "God, all things work together for good to those who love You. Enable us to learn important lessons from this situation so that we can get something good out of all the pain we have gone through. And please, pull us from this mess where we put ourselves and reunite our family."

Four and a half years later, David called me and told me of a job that was advertised online in the U.S. He told me to apply. I thought he was out of his mind. *A teaching job in the U.S advertised online, and I am in Kenya. This is crazy*. However, David insisted, so I applied. To my surprise, a few months later the director contacted me, and after several months of communication, I got the job. The director sent me a petition letter to take to the U.S. Embassy to request for a visa, and I was eventually granted a visa to come to the U.S. to teach.

Although I moved to Tennessee while my husband was in Texas, we visited each other whenever we could. But before reporting to work in Tennessee, I stayed with David for one month. It was then I realized that David and I had become so different that we needed to get to know each other all over again. It dawned on me that we needed to learn to live together again. Therefore, my being in Tennessee while David was in Texas gave us time to occasionally meet and discuss our values, priorities, and goals. We needed time to iron out our differences before we could live together "till death do us part." We needed to talk, apologize to each other, and forgive each other, which did not happen automatically. This was only achieved by God's grace and through much prayer.

As I reflected on our situation and the long separation, I appreciated the fact that I had come as a teacher and not a dependent of my husband as I had tried to do because the U.S. economy was taking a nosedive at the time. I thanked God for not giving me what I wanted only to give me something better. Also, though the distance between David and I was still uncomfortable, I was grateful that I had come to Advent Home where I was introduced to a vegan diet. As a result, I lost weight and improved my health.

This part of my life story reminds me of Joseph when he told his brothers, "But as for you, ye thought evil against me; but God meant it unto good, to bring to pass, as it is this day, to save much people alive" (Gen. 50:20). I believe that Satan instigated our separation for evil, but God allowed it, and out of the painful experience, we learned very important lessons in our lives. Personally, I don't know what other experience would have taught me to lose all confidence in myself and learn to depend on God completely.

In addition, during the time we were separated, both David and I realized how gracious God was to put us in each other's life. We now treasure our marriage and each other's company. We thank God for the institution of marriage. Also, we learned to forgive each other. During our separation, we hurt each other a great deal. During all the years we were separated, I developed strong bitterness. God instructed me to forgive, and I forgave David from my heart. In my bitterness, I did things that hurt David. He forgave me totally. When I see what is happening to the institution of marriage today, I know for sure my marriage is nothing but a miracle from God.

Chapter 11

In The Wilderness

Oh mercy! I thought I was a mature Christian. Did it have to take separating me from my husband and children for me to surrender fully to God? I pondered.

Before I came to teach in America, I had taught in Adventist schools in Kenya for more than twelve years. I had been a baptized member of the Seventh-day Adventist church for twenty-seven years. Within this time, I had held various positions in the church, and I thought I was a mature Christian and that I had totally surrendered my life to God. However, when I came to Advent Home, I experienced God in a very different way. As a missionary teacher in this self-supporting ministry, I developed very pressing needs. First, I missed my children whom I had left in Kenya and my husband who lived in Texas.

Secondly, for the most part, I was always in need of money. Advent Home could not afford to pay much because it is a self-supporting ministry that relies heavily on student fees. However, quite a good number of students could not pay due to financial difficulties on the part of their parents or guardians. The students were at-risk teen boys with such challenges as Attention Deficit Hyperactivity Disorder (ADHD), Oppositional Defiant Disorder (ODD), bipolar, impulsiveness, depression, school failure, substance abuse, and other dysfunctional behaviors. Although most of the students could not pay their tuition, they needed guidance and counseling, a lot of love, and many chances to work on their issues. Therefore, it was hard to send them away even when they could not pay. As a result, the staff had to sacrifice money and many other comforts to help these precious students.

For more than six months, I was not able to buy a cell phone because, to my shock, I could not walk into a shop, pay out money, and get a cell phone as I could do in Kenya. To get a cell phone, I needed a credit history—something I did not understand at all. As a result, communication with my people, both in America and in Kenya, was a big problem during that time.

Worse still, for more than two years, I was not able to buy a car. Therefore, I had to depend on colleagues to give me rides whenever I needed to go somewhere, which made me very dependent on other people. For the first few months at Advent Home, I longed for home, remembering how, while serving as a principal in Kenya, I received a car and travel allowance and a cell phone as part of my allowance and privileges from the school. I was used to being very independent. Now, I realized I had taken all those things for granted. I learned to thank God for things that, before then, I had not thought were worth thanking Him for.

However, as much as I felt uncomfortable being dependent on other people and being in need of money most of the time, God always provided everything I needed at the right time. This enhanced my faith and trust in Him.

As for my duties at Advent Home, I had to teach, counsel, and lead the students in worship despite their various needs due to their diverse disorders and various behavioral problems that had caused them to be kicked out of other schools. At first, handling these students was very challenging to me, because to deal with them successfully, I needed so much patience. To a significant extent, this had been a wanting trait in my life. In addition, I was used to making important decisions in the schools where I worked as an administrator. At Advent Home, I was a classroom teacher. Therefore, I had to take instructions from my supervisors. This humbled me—I loved the end result, but the process was painful sometimes.

All the same, the most difficult part of my duties came when I had to cook for both students and staff every third weekend of the month. First of all, I was not familiar with American dishes. The names of most ingredients were strange to me, and since I did not know the names for most foods, I could not follow the recipes. I liked cooking, and I wanted people to get delicious meals from me whenever it was my turn to work in the kitchen, but it was a struggle for me because of my background. Secondly, by the time I came to the U.S, I had employed house girls for eighteen years, which meant I hardly cooked my own food.

In the U.S., I worked many hours. I was overweight and sickly. Many times I had mixed feelings. On the one hand, I wanted to become active and independent so that I could live comfortably without house girls. On the other hand, I could get so tired and ask myself, *Do I really want to do this?* Furthermore, having left my children in Kenya made the situation very complicated. That made my life very stressful, especially during the first year. I often cried to God and asked for endurance and guidance.

Then one day, I had a dream. I saw a dove fly over me, and it stopped in the air in front of me. The dove looked at me with a very bright eye. As I was looking at it, admiring the bright eye (I could only see one eye since it faced me from one side), the whole dove transformed into one big bright human-like eye. The eye was brighter than the sun. I could not stare at it. In addition, the eye had both a reprimanding and an assuring look in it. After a minute or so of intently looking at me, it disappeared. Immediately after the eye disappeared, I woke up.

The dream left a strong impression on me that it was very important. I started praying and contemplating about the meaning of the dream. I asked God to reveal the meaning to me. Then toward the morning it came. A voice in my head told me that the dove represented God and that God had come to give me peace and assurance that He was with me and that I need not worry about my future or about my children.

Furthermore, the look also told me that God was not pleased with my anxiety and worry. My prolonged anxiety was a sign that I did not leave my problems totally in His hands. This showed a lack of trust and faith in God. I repented earnestly.

I asked God to give me the peace He had brought me. Once again, I asked God to keep my children in His mighty hands where I put them before I left Kenya. I prayed, "God of heaven, let nothing take my children from Your hands." Then I prayed that the Lord would increase my faith and trust in Him. I prayed for total surrender to His will.

From that day on, I experienced peace. And I never became depressed again about my children or my future. In a very clear mind, I prayed to God to open the way for me to go back to Kenya to see my children and to give me a green card so that I could either bring them over or go home freely to see them. I also asked Him to hasten the process of attaining the green card.

However, in spite of the difficulties at Advent Home, my experience there bore great dividends for me. I attained spiritual, academic, and social growth. Superficially, one would think that teaching at-risk boys would be all challenges and vexation. On the contrary, the blessings outweighed the challenges. My students at Advent Home, with their different special needs, attitudes, diverse potential, and interests, made me learn a very important lesson. I realized that, on my own, I could not teach or guide them.

Consequently, I learned to pray to God every day and during every single class period for God to send His Holy Spirit to take control of the class so that I could manage it and teach. I had to totally depend on God. I also realized that if I did not pray at the beginning of class and ask God for help I got very frustrated. Until I came to the U.S., I took my teaching for granted. I did not think it was a big thing to walk into a class and teach.

Furthermore, I learned to love my students regardless of what they did to me. I also learned to give them as many chances as possible. This experience improved my patience. In addition, as I helped the boys to identify and overcome their issues, I learned to look at myself objectively enough to realize my own issues that I needed to conquer by God's grace.

After spending several months at Advent Home, I said to myself, *I thought I was a mature Christian. I chose to teach in Adventist schools so that I could witness for God.* Just the same, after looking at my past life keenly, I realized that my desire to witness for God competed fervently with the desire to make money for my family. Several times, the desire to make money made me stay away from teaching to do business. But God always took me away from those businesses and put me back in school, either to further my education or to teach.

For some time, I exported *kiodos* (sisal baskets) from Nairobi to Tanzania and in return bought precious stones, Tanzanite and Rodlite, from Tanzania and sold them in Nairobi. At the same time, I exported tie-dye fabrics to South Africa, but in September 1998, I quit and went back to school to obtain a master's degree. For some reason, I despised money. I saw people get so much money so easily, and usually what they did with the money was drink and buy expensive clothes and jewelry. Within a few years, about half of my colleagues in this business died of AIDS. The only reason I am alive today is because I had Jesus in my life. God sustained me by His grace.

Furthermore, in March 2003 when I lost my job at the college I was teaching at, I started a taxi business in Machakos in Kenya. However, after a few months, I was impressed to go back to school to get a certificate in guidance and counseling. I enrolled at the University of Nairobi and obtained the certificate. Immediately after graduating, I started importing maize (corn) and beans from Uganda to sell in Kenya. There was a famine in Kenya, especially in my district, Makueni, and I bought the cereals and took them to the hungry people in the villages.

However, God removed me from this business and sent me to Kitui Adventist School where I became the principal after six months working as the deputy principal. To go back to teaching, I locked up my food store in Machakos town with more than 350 bags of maize and beans. This was worth several hundreds of thousands of shillings. When I went to Kitui, I did not ask how much I would be paid because I did not want to compare it to my previous paychecks. Later, I sent other people to sell the cereals for me so that I could hand over the store to the owner. I lost a lot of money in the process, but I was at peace because I knew I was doing what God wanted me to do by going back to teaching.

A few weeks after I arrived at Kitui Adventist School, two pastors and their wives came from Nairobi to see me. They told me, "Jonah, we can see you have arrived at Nineveh. We came to confirm that you are here so that we can bring you our children to teach them."

"I am here. Please bring them," I told them. They did indeed bring their children to Kitui Adventist School.

Well, at Advent Home I was pinned down by circumstances. As much as the salary was small, I could not start a business. The only thing my immigration documents allowed me to do was teach at the school. With the stress of being separated from family and having to operate with very little money, I got a chance to think clearly about my life and my relationship with God. With much prayer and soul searching, I began to understand what God had been trying to teach me over the years. Having been moved away from my distractions, I was able to hear God's voice—He had my full attention. Over the years I knew God wanted me to witness for Him. And by teaching in Adventist schools, I thought I was doing that. Little did I know that most of the time I had been witnessing for God on one hand and making money on the other hand. Furthermore, my eyes were opened, and I saw many habits that I needed to give up for me to experience God's power fully in my life.

Now, I knew that at Advent Home, I was in the wilderness to learn as Moses did. And I realized that I had to stay there for the whole period of time that God had set for me. Also, I remembered Nebuchadnezzar and what it took for him to humble himself before God. I sincerely repented, and by God's grace I reached the point to tell Him, "Lord, You are the potter; I am the clay. Make me what you have always wanted to make out of me."

However, to surrender total control of my life and my operations to God did not come easily. Many times I found myself making plans of what I wanted to do with my life without really consulting God about it. But God is so longsuffering. He kept reminding me all the time that I needed to let Him lead the way and that I could trust Him with my needs and my future.

Many times God allowed painful situations to happen. Then, I would remember that I had pushed Him out of the driver's seat. At this point, I realized that my desire to witness for God could not compete with the desire to make money. One had to occupy the first position in my life. On taking a keen flashback on my life, I realized that I had wasted a lot of precious time "chasing the wind" in the name of doing business. Yet, with all the businesses I operated, I saw a lot of money around me, but for some reason, it did not get into my pocket and make me rich. All I received was just enough for the needs of the family at the time. And I thank God for that.

All the same, I learned that surrender is not a one–time thing. As Ellen White says, "The precious graces of the Holy Spirit are not developed in a moment. Courage, fortitude, meekness, faith, unwavering trust in God's power to save, are acquired by the experience of years" (*Mind, Character, and Personality*, vol. 1, p. 17).

I realized the need to surrender every day. And with much prayer and total surrender of my will to God's will, making money and creating wealth for my family became less important. I became preoccupied with the desire to witness. All the focus moved from me and my family to other people. Winning souls for Christ became my number one concern. It was then that I began to experience peace I had never known in my life.

I am very grateful for the lessons I learned since I came to America and especially to Advent Home. Although this was a real desert for me, I prayed, "Lord, please help me to learn all the lessons that I came here to learn." I thought about Moses in the wilderness for forty years, and this story encouraged me. Now I thank God for moving me from my comfort zone in Kenya to the U.S. so that I could learn the purpose of my life. I have learned that as long as I am following God's purpose for my life I have peace and joy, since He provides the wisdom, strength, and resources to do the work. In fact, writing this book is one of the blessings of discovering God's purpose for my life.

This reminds me that no matter how messed up my situation is, God is able to pull together all the pieces to enable me to say, surely, "All things work together for good to them that love God, to them who are the called according to his purpose" (Rom. 8:28).

Chapter 12

God Rescued Me From Satan's Attack

What are you doing here? You are such a failure in life. See how much you miss your children and husband. Your family is so scattered. How will you ever reunite? On and on the voice in my head kept nagging and taunting me, reminding me of the situation of my family and all the things I ever wanted to do in life but would never get a chance to do.

It was July 21, 2008, a little over one year since I had come to the U.S., and I missed my children very much. On this Saturday evening, I decided to watch a video I had taken of my beloved children before I came to the U.S. It was a video of the children talking, singing, and playing together. At the time, I was preparing to come to the U.S. in two weeks' time. My daughter was going to her boarding school the following day. Therefore, I cooked our favorite meal: chapatti, ugali, cabbage, and meat-stew so that we could enjoy eating together. The delicious-smelling food filled the whole house with a pleasant aroma. The two children ate as they joked with each other. Their happy mood was infectious though the thought of leaving them in Kenya as I came to the U.S. was very heavy on me. For six months since I had been given the visa to come to the U.S., I often was deep in thought.

After eating, I told the two teenagers to sing their favorite songs. Then they started scratching their heads trying to remember the songs they sang together in their Pathfinder classes and those they sang together at Maxwell Adventist School before they went to different high schools. After they were done with primary school songs, they went on to sing songs they had sung in church as teenagers. They did a good job apart from when they decided to sing my favorite songs, trying to imitate me. As I watched the video, I occasionally burst out laughing. For instance, at one point, my daughter put on my hat and incited her brother to sing one of my favorite songs then:

I will call upon the Lord who is worthy to be praised.

So shall I be safe from the enemy,

I will call upon the Lord.

The Lord liveth and blessed be the rock

and the rock of my salvation be exalted.

The Lord liveth and blessed be the rock

and the rock of my salvation be exalted.

I liked leading students in singing this song in church before I greeted them. So, my children imitated my voice in singing the song and then greeted imaginary students at the same time adjusting imaginary spectacles before they both collapsed, cracking their ribs in laughter. Although I told them to stop playing and be serious, I was amused. Watching this video more than a year later gave me a mixed feeling. I was amused, but at the same time I felt a deep nostalgia for home. My children always made me happy. After singing for some time, I called the children to sit down so we could talk.

Then I asked them, "How do you feel about my going to America?"

"It's okay because you are going to see Dad. But we will miss you," my son said.

"I don't want to think about it. I don't know how it will be. I can't imagine not seeing you for a year, Mom. I don't know when we will see each other next. But I really want you to go because of Dad," said Lulu.

"As far as I am concerned, I know next year I am going to the university, and even if you were here, we would have to meet occasionally. But for Lulu it is different because she is a girl, and she is still young. Anyway, because of Dad, go well, Mom," said Wisdom.

When my children started talking about my going to America, their demeanor changed from the joyous playful mood to one of seriousness and almost sadness. However, they both were willing to sacrifice their comfort for the sake of reuniting their parents. After they said all they wanted to say, my turn came.

Then I started, "My children, this issue has been so heavy on my heart. It has been a very difficult decision for me to make. It has been six months since I received the visa to go teach in America. I am going as a missionary to teach at-risk teen boys who have different disorders and behavioral problems. I really would like to make a difference in a young person's life. I will also be able to be united with your father after these five and a half years. While I will be united with your father, I will be separated from you by distance. I know we will miss each other, but it will be for a short time because God will open a way for us to be united as a family again. One thing I want to tell you now is to always remember to live in the fear of the Lord as you have always done." On and on I told them things they should not forget in their lives.

After sharing all the advice with my children before I left them, I wondered whether they still remembered and followed the teachings or not. Whenever those thoughts came to my mind, I remembered the dream about the dove where God reminded me to trust Him with all my cares. I prayed as I always did, "Lord, please keep my children in Your mighty hands where I left them. Let nothing take them from Your hands. In the name of Jesus, I pray. Amen."

The video went on to feature Masii SDA Secondary School choir singing on a Sabbath afternoon. This is the school where I had been principal just before I came to the U.S. I missed the students too, but I enjoyed their singing, so I continued to watch. All of a sudden, a voice started whispering the most discouraging and mean words I had ever heard in my life. Then my mood changed immediately. I felt disappointed, frustrated, and very depressed. I was in this state for more than two hours. It was getting close to midnight, but I was unable to stand up and walk up the stairs to my bedroom to go to sleep.

I needed to read for a course I was taking online for my teaching certification, but I felt too discouraged to read. I decided to go upstairs, pray, and force myself to sleep. I went up and knelt down beside my bed to pray. But instead of praying, my mind began viewing all my failures again. This time the voice in my head told me how miserable I was even at work. For some time, I knelt there, but I was unable to pray. The voice in my mind would not give me the chance, and I seemed to have no control over it.

Then, all of a sudden I gained strength, and I heard myself rebuking Satan. At the same time, another voice in my mind asked me, *What don't you have? What don't you have in life?* I continued praying, thanking God for His love for me and for giving me children, a husband, a job, and good health for the whole family. I prayed for God to defeat Satan in my life and that all the wiles of the evil one and his agents would be defeated. In the name of Jesus Christ, I prayed with such power that it shocked me. I felt myself in a state that was beyond my control. I got scared, climbed into my bed, and lay there, tired and shocked.

After some time, it dawned on me that all the time my mind was nagging and taunting me, showing me all my failures in this life, I was under the attack of Satan. But God, in His love and tender mercy, did not allow the devil to traumatize me beyond what I could withstand. At the right time, I received help. God must have sent an angel to come to my rescue. I trembled in my bed. The atmosphere in my bedroom felt very tense. I felt as if there was an argument in the darkness. When I regained calmness, I did not know how to thank God for rescuing me from this strong attack of Satan.

This was the second time Satan had attacked me so directly. The first time was in 1989. I was eight months pregnant with my son, Wisdom. This time my husband and I were teaching at Mutitu SDA Secondary School. The teachers' houses were built with bathrooms outside the houses, and the bathrooms were built on a hilly place. To go up to them, we had to climb some dirt stairs almost ten feet above the ground. Next to the dirt stairs was a fallen dry tree with sharp, protruding sword-like branches.

Every day we went up and down the dirt stairs without giving much thought to the fallen tree. However, one day I came out of the bathroom and stood for a second to prepare myself to come down the stairs carefully since I was very heavy with a child. But before I could take my first step, I was pushed from behind directly toward the dry tree with my belly facing the sharp sword-like branches on the ground. I screamed. Miraculously, I was instantly held in the air and carried over the tree branches. I landed gently on my feet without getting hurt at all.

However, when I stood back on my feet, I had mixed feelings. A part

God Rescued Me From Satan's Attack

of me was shocked because when I came out of the bathroom I did not see anybody around. Whatever shoved me was unseen. I just felt myself pushed from behind, and I knew for sure that either Satan or his angel had pushed me from the raised ground toward the fallen dry tree below. I could not understand why Satan was so enraged with me. On the other hand, I was overjoyed by God's care and protection. I could not comprehend the instant rescue from the death that Satan had planned for me and my unborn baby. Then I experienced the truth that, "The angel of the LORD encampeth round about them that fear him" (Ps. 34:7). David and I could not thank God enough for His sustaining mercies.

The following week my mother came to visit us. After two days of her stay with us, she noticed that every time she entered our bathroom she heard a puppy crying outside the bathroom. But whenever she came out, she could not see any puppy or anything else around. After several similar experiences, she decided to take a flashlight to the toilet to look for whatever cried like a puppy all the time. To her shock, she saw a big pig in the toilet. She came back to the house to get us. The pig looked so big, with a long tail that looked artificial at the end.

In amazement we stared at the pig, wondering how on earth it had gotten inside the toilet. First of all, no living thing survives in a toilet for days. Secondly, nobody in our area kept pigs! Mother told us that it must have been a devil in the form of a pig. Well, we prayed and asked God to continue protecting us from harm; then, we continued with our lives as if nothing had happened.

Just the same, seeing the pig was the beginning of Satan's attacks on me. A few days later David was building a chicken house outside. I stood two steps from him when I was pushed violently against the chicken house. A protruding nail caught my left leg and pierced deep into my flesh. This time I was so scared and traumatized that I had to be taken to the hospital in shock. David and I did not know what the devil was going to do next, but we continued praying, and soon we were calm and peaceful. However, I still have the scar on my left leg to this day, and the scar tells me how much Satan hates me. The scar is a constant reminder that Satan is an enemy. All the same, Satan was not yet done with me.

God Makes a Way

Two weeks later when it was time to deliver my baby, I had another close encounter with death. After I delivered the baby in Machakos Nursing Home, the nurses who helped me did not notice that part of the placenta remained in my womb. I delivered at 3:00 a.m. By 7:00 a.m. the following morning, I had lost a lot of blood. This was my first delivery, and I knew it was normal to lose blood. But I did not know that I was bleeding too much. Furthermore, it was at night, so immediately after I delivered, I slept. In the morning when I tried to stand up, I passed out and remained unconscious for the whole day. Several doctors from different hospitals in Machakos resuscitated me. They removed the remaining piece of placenta and gave me several pints of blood in a transfusion. I regained consciousness late in the evening.

At this point, many people realized that my life was in danger, and they prayed for me so much that Satan left me alone for some time. Going through these experiences gave me strength and courage to persevere during difficult situations later on. Whenever I went through very trying moments, I always looked back to this time when it looked as if all I had in life were trials, temptations, and torture from the devil. Yet, it passed, and I was left stronger than before. This time I proved James 4:7 to be true "Submit yourselves therefore to God. Resist the devil, and he will flee from you."

Chapter 13

Incredible Flight From Chattanooga to Houston

In December 2008 we closed school for Christmas break. During such breaks I left Advent Home in Tennessee and went to Houston, Texas, to spend time with David. David, too, would come to visit me whenever he could. We always looked forward to such times when we could get a chance to be together. In addition, I always enjoyed taking breaks from Advent Home because sometimes it would get stressful dealing with new students before they reached a point where they could start cooperating with the program.

These new students would come with disorders like ADHD, bipolar, or behavioral problems. Once at school they would be introduced to a vegan diet, work program, and discipline that most of them did not have in their homes. At first, new students acted out, defying instruction and refusing to work with the program. During such times it caused more work for staff, and most of the time, the situation was stressful for both students and staff. Hence, whenever a break was possible, we welcomed the opportunity to calm our nerves and to recuperate.

This particular time, I flew from Chattanooga, Tennessee, to Bush International Airport in Houston, Texas. That day the weather was very bad. It had rained heavily, and there was fog everywhere, especially between Bowater in Calhoun and Chattanooga. Two colleagues accompanied me to the airport. As we drove, we talked and discussed various issues. However, at the back of my mind, I was concerned about the bad weather because many flights had been delayed in various airports due to the bad weather. I did not want my flight to be delayed or, at worst, to be cancelled—I only had a few days of vacation. Therefore, one part of me was conversing with my colleagues while the other part was praying in my heart for my trip.

Soon we arrived at the airport, and I bade my colleagues goodbye as I went to check in my bags. As I sat waiting for the boarding time, I continued to pray for the trip. At last, the time came for us to board the plane. My seat was next to a window. Upon taking off, I wondered how the pilot could get us to Houston because, though it was daytime, I could not see anything through the window. There was total darkness in the sky. It looked as if heavy, dark clouds had covered the whole country. The flight was the roughest I had ever experienced.

After taking off, I felt as if the pilot was shooting straight into the sky, and after a few minutes, the plane went up above the clouds. Way above the heavy clouds the weather was very clear. Looking through the window, the clouds that had looked so dark and which had scared me before now looked so beautiful. Looking at them from above, they looked like snow or like one long sheet of soft cotton. The gorgeous looking clouds seemed to form hills and valleys of very elegant fleece. But when the plane was flying through them, they looked so dark. *Why was I so scared of the clouds before?* I wondered. *I'm glad the pilot did not fly through the dark clouds for long.*

After I relaxed I started thinking of other situations in life where I had been so scared and worried about things that had never come to pass. I thought, *Suppose people were able to rise above their daily problems? Suppose people were able to see with their eyes of faith and penetrate the heavy clouds of divorce, sickness, loneliness, poverty, and many other situations that they find themselves in.*

As I looked out the window, my eyes stayed fixed on the fleecy clouds below, but my mind fixated on all the problems that throw men, women, and youth to despair. Then my mind switched to my students, and I could not help thinking of the low self-esteem that many of them struggled with. In a flash, I remembered all the cases I had been dealing with in my students: suicidal thoughts, depression, low academic achievement, inferiority complex, disobedience, poor relationships, etc.

I thought about the causes of low self-esteem: social, economical, physical, etc. From my analysis, I could see that some of the causes were beyond the person's control. Then I thought, suppose these people, young and old, could focus their attention not on their problems but on the power beyond the clouds. What if these people could look up with eyes of faith that can penetrate the clouds and see God in their minds; what difference would it make?

Occasionally, I gave my fellow travelers a sweeping look and wondered what each one of them was thinking about. Then I thought about the power of positive thinking and the peace that comes when one surrenders all to the Lord. Immediately verses started unwrapping themselves in my mind: "Be careful for nothing; but in every thing by prayer and supplication with thanksgiving let your requests be made known unto God" (Phil. 4:6). I then thought of Jeremiah 33:3: "Call unto me, and I will answer thee, and show thee great and mighty things, which thou knowest not." Almost every serious Christian has a Bible, so these verses are not new to them. Unfortunately, many of these Christians are languishing in despair because of problems that they believe are impossible for anybody to solve. I wondered, *Does anything puzzle God?*

As if my thoughts wanted to provide an answer to my question, they turned to me, and I remembered a time when I had become very anxious and stressed. One year earlier, in December 2007, my two teenage children had traveled from Nairobi to Kisumu to visit their Aunt Carol and Uncle Patrick and their cousins who had invited them over for the Christmas holidays. Kisumu is in the territory of the Luo people. My family and I belong to the Kamba tribe. When the civil war broke between a few tribes of Kenya, my children and my sister-in-law's family found themselves in danger because they were in the middle of the warring tribes.

One day somebody informed my sister-in-law and her husband that people were going to attack them that evening. My children and their relatives got very scared and moved to a pastor's house in the town. My children called me and my husband from the pastor's home and informed us that they were hiding there.

A day later they called again and told us that people had told the pastor that they knew he was hiding people from other tribes in his house. They threatened to burn down his house that evening. At this point, my sister-in-law and her husband called the police and requested an escort to move out of the city of Kisumu to Kakamega, which was the nearest town where there was no fighting. My brother-in-law had a friend there; hence it was the only place they could go to hide. They could not find their way home because all other routes were blocked by tribal warriors. All this time, I was in Houston where I had gone to visit my husband. We hardly ate or slept for a while. We called the children and our relatives every few minutes to find out whether they were still alive. We earnestly prayed to God to save our children and relatives. This is a time when we experienced a great amount of fear, anxiety, and stress.

Hundreds of people lost their lives in Kenya during this time. But God shielded my children and their hosts until they reached Kakamega where they hid. After a few days, we were able to make arrangements so that the children could fly to Nairobi and be safely taken out of the city, which was also very dangerous by then. The family of my sister-in-law remained in Kakamega until it was safe for them to return to their home in Kisumu.

By the time my mind was done reminding me of all this, I realized that people do not have to be non-Christians to be scared, stressed, and even depressed. Most of the time, we give God our problems, but our faith is not strong enough to enable us to leave the problems in God's hands and relax. Many times we take back our problems from God's hands. That is when anxiety, stress, and depression occur.

"If we educated our souls to have more faith, more love, greater patience, a more perfect trust in our heavenly Father, we would have more peace and happiness as we pass through the conflicts of this life. The Lord is not pleased to have us fret and worry ourselves out of the arms of Jesus" (Ellen G. White, *Mind, Character, and Personality*, vol. 2, p. 468).

One of the verses that I remembered at this point was Mark 11:24 where Jesus said, "Therefore I say unto you, What things soever ye desire, when ye pray, believe that ye receive them, and ye shall have them."

By the time the flight attendant announced that we were a few minutes from Houston and should prepare ourselves for landing, I was so excited about my thoughts that I had written a few lines in my notebook.

Although I had not planned to write a book, I prayed for an opportunity to share my thoughts with other people to encourage them just as I had been encouraged by the thought of giving our problems to God by faith and trusting in His will. This attitude takes constant prayer and reading of the Word of God so that we can learn to claim God's promises in every difficult situation.

Chapter 14

Witnessing at Advent Home

In the second week of February 2009, the principal of Advent Home Learning Center told me that I was the one to conduct morning worship for the students the following week. Immediately after she told me that, my mind went straight to a topic I was contemplating as I had been dealing with some personal issues that month. The topic was "God Makes a Way."

Since January I had been dealing with issues concerning changing my immigration status. A few weeks before this time, my director had received a letter from immigration asking for proof that I was a genuine religious worker. When he gave me the letter, I went home and cried.

I cried out to the Lord, "God, who knows that I am truly a religious worker and a missionary teacher or a minister apart from You? Yes, for many years I have taught in church schools. For many years I have served in various churches. But whom have I been serving? Was I always motivated by a desire to serve You without some selfish motives?"

After asking all these questions, my whole life opened up before me like a book. I could see that many times God had led me to achieve great success in the schools where I had taught and administered, but I also saw that many times I had failed to bring glory to the name of God. I cried bitterly. Then a voice asked me, "Why do you want a green card? Do you want it so that you can serve God freely in America and in African countries, or do you want it so that you can move and get a better paying job in America?"

At this point, I became alert like somebody who had just washed her face with cold water. For a minute, I did not know exactly why I wanted a green card. I knew my R1 visa was expiring in a few months and that I wanted to

85

continue teaching at Advent Home for some time, but beyond that I did not know exactly why I wanted a green card. To the asking voice, I said, "I don't know."

The voice in me said, "Search yourself and write your reasons down." After one or two days, I realized that I needed the green card so that I could serve God both in America and Africa, especially in Kenya. I realized I would need to travel back and forth. So, I wrote it down. Since that day God took charge of the course of the processing of my green card.

There was no single stage of that process that God did not inform me about what was going to happen beforehand. Besides, the process went so fast that my colleagues wondered about it. All I could tell them was that God was doing everything for me. Immediately after the I-360, petition for immigrants to the U.S., was approved, laws changed, and it became very hard for immigrants to the U.S. to get green cards through R1 visas. My lawyer's legal assistant called me and told me that chances of me getting the green card were almost zero. She told me that if I applied for an I-485, application to register permanent residence in the U.S., I risked losing a lot of money for nothing.

I wrote an e-mail to the lawyer and said, "I am sending you your fee. I have faith; please do your job. I am not asking for this document from anybody. I am asking for it from God. If God decides to give it to me, nobody will thwart Him." I promised to send my lawyer $1,810 for himself and the USCIS (U.S Citizenship and Immigration Services). On receiving this e-mail, my lawyer sent me the forms to apply for the I-485. So I needed to send the $1,810 immediately, but I did not have it

Then I went to my director's office and told him that I needed money. The organization had just laid off eight people due to lack of funds. However, the director wrote me a note to take to the accountant instructing her to give me the money but warning me that the account could be lacking that kind of money.

All the same, I got the money and paid for the I-485. After collecting all the needed documents, I took them in person to the lawyer's office where I got a chance to sit down and talk to the legal assistant. She told me that the whole office was awed by the way my case was proceeding and especially considering that, in those days, it was very hard for anybody to get a green card from a R1 visa. However, my case seemed to be heading in the direction of approval. "Nobody thwarts the God of heaven," I told her.

Two weeks after turning in my application, I received a letter informing me that my I-485 had been approved and that I needed to go for biometrics. I did and waited confidently for God to make a way for me.

It was after this experience that my principal asked me to conduct morning worship for the students. No wonder the only topic that was ringing in my mind was "God Makes a Way." I based the first day's talk on Exodus 13:17 to Exodus 14. I placed emphasis on chapter 14, verse 13: "And Moses said unto the people, Fear ye not, stand still, and see the salvation of the LORD, which he will shew to you to day." Verse 22 says, "And the children of Israel went into the midst of the sea upon the dry ground: and the waters were a wall unto them on their right hand, and on their left."

I asked the students to share experiences of times when they found themselves between the devil and the deep seas, as the old saying goes. Because Advent Home was a special school for at-risk teen boys, most of the students had gone through experiences that were difficult. But none of them had ever found himself in a worse situation than the Israelites at the time God parted the Red Sea for them to escape from the Egyptians. The conclusion this day was that the God who had made a way for the Israelites through the Red Sea is the same God we worship today. So we do not need to fear. All we need to do is stand still on our faith and ask God to make a way for us. God did it in the past; He is able to do it today.

The second day we studied Ezra 8. Ezra 8 is one of the chapters of the Bible that I have read many times. Some of the ideas that intrigue me so much in this chapter are in verses 21 to 23 and verses 31 to 33. I find it interesting that Ezra was ashamed to ask for an escort from the king because he had spoken to the king saying, "'The hand of our God is upon all them for good that seek him; but his power and his wrath is against all them that forsake him' (Ezra 8:22). Therefore, Ezra proclaimed a fast and asked the people to humble themselves before the Lord to seek of Him a right way for the people, their children and their possessions."

I asked my students to think about some of the situations that they found shameful as Christians. Some said they found it shameful to fail exams after praying. Others said as Christians they were ashamed when they were unable to overcome their issues of anger or fighting.

Lastly, it was my turn to share, and I told them that many times I find myself in a situation that makes me remember Ezra's experience. One of these times came when I was the principal of Kitui Adventist School in Kenya. The eighth grade students had written their final national exam, and when the results came out, many students had done well, but a neighboring school had done better than our school. As a result, some people decided to mock our school. The deputy principal of the primary school told me that people were saying, "The Adventist school is always praying. Why didn't they do better than other schools?" When I heard this, I wept. Then I called all the teachers together for a meeting to encourage them. I told them to focus their minds on God and their work. We prayed, and many of us fasted and prayed for our school.

The following year our school did very well. Many students achieved A's in several subjects. In addition, God answered my prayers in two ways. First, the whole school did well, and many students were admitted to both provincial and national schools, which is the dream of many parents and students in Kenya. Secondly, my daughter was one of the students who did very well. We expected her to receive a high score, but personally, I knew it was God's doing for her to do that well, even in math. She had always struggled with math. One and a half months later, high school national exam results (KCSE) came out too, and my son had also done very well. I found God very faithful because my children and I had placed all our hope in the mighty hands of God.

Before we ended our worship that morning, one of the students read Ezra 8:31: "Then we departed from the river of Ahava on the twelfth day of the first month, to go unto Jerusalem: and the hand of our God was upon us, and he delivered us from the hand of the enemy, and of such as lay in wait by the way." We noted that Ezra's prayer together with other Israelites was answered by God. God made a way for them from Babylon to Jerusalem as they desired. Sometimes we pray, but we do not receive what we ask for. Then we wonder why it is that God did not give us what we asked from Him. We decided to analyze the situation of Ezra and the Israelites when they prayed.

On the third and the fourth day we studied the case of Ezra and the Israelites, which is found in Ezra 8, in detail. First, we noted that the Israelites, under the guidance of Ezra, humbled themselves before the Lord. They fasted and pleaded with the Lord. We were interested to find out what it means to humble oneself before the Lord. We used the Bible to define itself, so we read from Philippians 2:8: "And being found in fashion as a man, he humbled himself, and became obedient unto death, even the death of the cross. Wherefore God also has highly exalted him, and given him a name which is above every name." From this verse my students noted that to humble oneself to the Lord means obedience to God's will, just as Jesus humbled Himself even to death.

Next we read, "If my people, which are called by my name, shall humble themselves, and pray, and seek my face, and turn from their wicked ways; then will I hear from heaven, and will forgive their sins, and will heal their land" (2 Chron. 7:14). At this point, I pointed out to my students that for one to truly humble oneself before the Lord means to turn away from doing wickedness, repent of one's sins, and recognize the Lord as God and Lord of one's life. Then God will answer your prayers. In conclusion, we read James 4:3: "Ye ask, and receive not, because ye ask amiss, that ye may consume it upon your lusts."

The fifth day was our last day on the topic. I asked the students what they understood by the title of our sermon for the week. One student said, "What I understand by our title, *God Makes a Way*, is that God is able to deliver His people from any trouble or from any situation."

Another student said, "God is able to create a way to save His people from any situation."

On the last day, we read from 2 Chronicles 20. Here we saw how God fought for Judah when a great multitude of the children of Moab and Ammon came together to fight against them. Just like Ezra, Jehoshaphat proclaimed a fast to seek the Lord's guidance. And after fasting and crying to the Lord, the Spirit of the Lord told the people of Judah, "Be not afraid nor dismayed by reason of this great multitude; for the battle is not yours, but God's" (verse 15).

From verse 20 to 24 we saw how the people of Judah defeated the great multitude by simply singing and shouting praises to the Lord. The multitudes killed one another and none escaped. God made a way for the people of Judah. On their own they could not fight such a big multitude, but with God they did not need to raise a spear. In our discussion some students mentioned the way the Israelites conquered the city of Jericho.

God Makes a Way

To sum up our discussion for the whole week, we concluded that surely God makes a way. So long as we humble ourselves and totally surrender to Him, He fights for us to overcome evil. Whatever we ask He gives us so long as it will bring glory to Him. Just the same, we need to realize that God loves us more than we love ourselves, and He knows what is best for us. Therefore, we must trust Him regardless of our situations in life. Also, we read, "But God is faithful, who will not suffer you to be tempted above that ye are able; but will with the temptation also make a way to escape, that ye may be able to bear it" (1 Cor. 10:13).

Chapter 15

Miracle Ticket to Kenya

"You need to pay four hundred and forty dollars to the government for your taxes," the officer calculating my tax returns informed me.

"Do you mean I am the one to pay the government money?" I asked.

"Yes," the officer informed me.

I went silent for a few seconds taking in what she had just said before I finally asked why.

The lady tried to explain that I had not been paying anything for federal taxes—that was why I was the one to pay, not the other way around. I stretched out my hand to collect my documents from her. I needed to go back to school and think through my situation. It was hard to understand why I could not get anything from taxes that year when I had worked the whole year. And besides, I had so many tax-deductible receipts. I expected to receive around three thousand dollars from my tax returns. Well, I did not understand how the tax returns were calculated. I had receipts totaling about three thousand dollars, and I thought I would receive the whole amount.

All the same, I planned to use the three thousand dollars I expected to receive from taxes to pay for an airplane ticket to Kenya to see my children and parents, especially my father who was more than a hundred years old. This was around February 2009, and I knew that I could not save a coin for my trip between then and June because I had financial obligations that did not allow me to save any significant amount of money. I had high hopes in the tax returns only to find out that, instead of getting money from the government, I had a debt, and I did not know what to do.

For a few days, I felt lost. I did not have any hope of getting money from

God Makes a Way

anywhere else. Yet going back to Kenya was absolutely necessary; it was compulsory because my daughter was on the verge of breaking down. She so badly wanted to see me, and I too missed my children very much. Having been separated from them for two years, I needed to go home and sit down with them and guide them as young people.

Up to the month of May, I still did not have money for the ticket. One Sabbath I felt sick and did not go to church. In the afternoon, three ladies, my colleague and two prayer partners, realized that I had not been at church. They called me to find out whether I was well. I told them I felt sick. They all came to pray with me. Before we prayed one of them asked me, "Are you worried or stressed about anything?"

"I don't know whether I am worried about anything or not. All I know is that this is the month of May, and I need to go to Kenya in July to see my children," I said. "Up to now, I do not have money, and I have no plans on how to raise money for the ticket. However, I thought I was just concerned; I did not know that I was worried about it."

"I can see that you are stressed about something. Ms. Susan," she said. "You have been preaching to the students that 'God makes a way.' Do you think your ticket to Kenya is too much for God? How much do you need to go to Kenya?"

"At least three thousand dollars," I said. We talked back and forth for a little bit. Then it was time for us to pray. I was the first to pray, and in my prayer I repented for being anxious about the money for the trip. I asked God to help my unbelief. All the other ladies prayed for my healing and for God to provide for all my needs, including my trip.

When the time came for the sister who had asked me whether I was worried about something to pray, this is what she said: "Lord God, I am ashamed for Ms. Susan. She is worried about three thousand dollars to go to Kenya. It is important for her to go home to see her children because they have been separated for a long time, but she has no reason to get worried and stressed about it. She has been preaching to the boys that You can make a way, even where humanly speaking there is no way. And, Lord, look at what You just did for her. You got her green card approved when other workers had to leave their jobs here and go back to their countries in tears. You led her to get her green card so fast when other people here were denied the same. Please, Lord, forgive Ms. Susan and help her unbelief. Teach her to learn to fully trust You, to give You all her burdens, and to stop taking them back to herself. In the name of Jesus Christ our Savior, we pray."

We all said, "Amen."

When the ladies left, I had a moment of self-searching. I asked myself, *Do I believe what I preach to others, or is it easier to encourage other people to trust God in all situations without believing it myself?* For a moment I felt ashamed. Surely God had been so gracious to me in so many ways. This sister knew the details of the way God was dealing with me, so tenderly and kindly in a very miraculous way. For a moment, I thought of the children of Israel and their perpetual murmuring against God whenever He allowed any temptation to befall them.

The Israelites forgot about all the miracles God had used to save them from the Egyptians and how He had provided for their needs in the wilderness and blamed Him all the time for taking them out of Egypt. I once again repented, and from that time on, I decided to trust God with my trip. Then I prayed, "God, it is impossible for me to raise all the money I need for my trip, but I leave it in Your hands. You are God and nothing puzzles You. Please organize my trip for me and provide everything I need to comfortably go on this trip. In the name of Jesus Christ my Savior, I pray. Amen."

A week from that day, Ms. Elsie, one of the ladies who had come to pray for me, got a new job where she earned much more money than what she was getting at our self-supporting ministry. She came to my office one morning and told me she would help raise money for my ticket to Kenya. I thought I did not hear properly. She told me, "Yes, I will help you." The following week, she gave me a check for $750. Then David sent me $800 check, and my director gave me a pay advance for $1,000. I received my salary for the month of June, which was $1,154, and by God's grace I did not need to send my children any money at that time.

By mid-June I was able to pay for my air ticket, which I got at $1,470 at a time when all cheap flights were going at $1,760. I sang and sang praises to God. I knew God had made a way for me. However, my joy was short-lived. Two weeks before my travel date, I talked to my brother-in-law Samuel and told him how excited I was because I was going home to see my children in two weeks' time. On hearing this he told me, "I thought your I-485 is pending in the immigration office."

"Yes, what about it?" I asked.

"You cannot go out of the country when your green card is pending," he said. "If you go the immigration office will drop your application. Talk to your lawyer about it."

I called my lawyer and talked to the legal assistant who told me that I could safely travel using my valid R1 visa. However, I decided to call the immigration office where my I-485 was pending. To my shock, the officer who answered the phone told me, "If your I-485 is pending, you need advance parole, a travel document, to travel out of the country. If you go without it, your application will be dropped."

"How long does it take to get an advance parole?" I asked.

"Advance parole takes two to three months," he said. "However, you can get one in five days if you have a real emergency. You need to call the nearest immigration office and book an appointment to go and present your case."

By this time I had precisely two weeks to my departure date. I went straight to my computer to search for the immigration offices in my region. The nearest was in Atlanta. I tried to book an appointment online, which was the only way to get an appointment for the interview, but I found that there were no openings for the next three weeks. *My flight is in two weeks' time. I don't have three weeks to wait for the advance parole interview appointment.*

If I missed my flight two weeks from then, there would be no refund. For a moment, I thought about how hard it was for me to raise the money for my ticket. I got annoyed with my lawyer whose advice I had sought several months before and whose legal assistant kept telling me that I could travel on my R1 visa, even though my I-485 was pending.

Furthermore, at the time I had applied for the I-485, I had paid for both advance parole and a work permit, but my lawyer had not processed the documents for me. On asking why he told me that I did not sent him passport size photos. Nobody had asked me to send my photos.

But I did not have time to be annoyed or to quarrel. I needed to forgive so that I could think clearly and rely on God. I talked to my colleagues and told them that it seemed that I could not go on my trip as I had expected because I needed three months to get an advance parole, unless I had an emergency in which case I could get it in five working days. One of my colleagues told me that my going out of the country would still affect the processing of my green card negatively, whether I got the advance parole or not. My going would prolong the duration of processing the document.

I felt so confused. It was 6:00 p.m., time for supper. I left my office and stood outside the building. I watched students and staff streaming to the two dorms where we ate, but I did not feel hungry. After standing for some time staring at God's creation without focusing on anything in particular, I slowly walked to my apartment. The only thing that came into my mind was to cry to God, so I prayed and told Him, "Father, I don't know what You are going to do, but I know nothing puzzles You. If it is Your will, please, make a way for me to go home."

I felt both mentally and physically drained. I had spent the whole day thinking, planning, and pleading with God. I needed to rest. I prayed for a peaceful night's rest, and I went to sleep.

I woke up early the next morning well rested but still feeling a bit overwhelmed. However, there was a calm voice telling me not to give up. Every time I thought *maybe this trip was not meant to be*, the voice would firmly tell me, "Susana, don't give up."

I struggled with different thoughts as I kept wondering why I had prayed and struggled so much to make this trip happen only to meet such heavy obstacles. *Does God want me to go? Suppose the thugs who threatened to kill me before I left home still want to kill me?* In spite of these scary thoughts, I felt a very deep longing for home. I missed my mother and wished I could see her and sit down with her to share my experiences. I knew my mother always worried about me, especially since I had come to the U.S. To her, America was like another planet. None of her children had ever gone so far away from home.

I decided to call her. A few minutes after dialing her cell phone number, I heard her voice.

"Hello, hello. Susana, *mwanaakwa, wakya*?" (Susana, my child, how are you?)

Her voice was full of joy and excitement to hear my voice. She always was excited whenever I called her. I could hear the sigh of relief as if to say, *Thank you, God, my child is still alive in that foreign land.*

"I'm doing well, Mom. How is everybody?" I asked.

"We are all well apart from your father who has been sick for the past week. He refuses to eat, and he does not want to be taken to the hospital," she told me.

"What exactly is the problem?" I asked.

"I don't know. He is just not happy. He sleeps all day and refuses to eat. Living in this world for over one hundred years is not a joke. He tells me that he is going all the time," Mom said.

"Where does he say he is going?" I asked.

"He never answers that," she said.

"Where does he say he feels pain?" I asked.

"All over his body," said Mom.

"I will organize for him to be taken to the hospital," I told my mother.

Father was more than one hundred years old, and he rarely got sick. Apart from his teeth that had bothered him when he was around sixty years old and had all been taken out and replaced with dentures, he was never ill. The next time he was sick he had caught a cold and some skin rash around the neck when he was around one hundred years old, but then, whenever he felt some slight pain in his body, he thought it was time for him to follow all of his friends to the grave. At this age, he did not process things well. For example, apart from me, he did not remember his other children. Whenever my siblings went home, he would ask them, "Who are you?"

My sibling would respond, "I am your child."

"Which one?" he would ask. Then my sibling would tell his or her name. After he heard their name, my father would remember them and start asking relevant questions about their family or work. Then he would give them relevant advice depending on whatever he felt was necessary for them to know.

All the same, Father refused to be rushed to the hospital every time he felt pain because he said that nobody could treat and heal old age. He used to ask us to identify any of his friends who were still living. Honestly, we could not think of one. Then he would tell us that he too would follow them and no doctor could prevent him from going when the time came. Most of the time, whenever he started talking like this, people would think that he was out of his mind. My siblings would get scared.

Even before I came to the U.S., I lived far from home. And whenever I went home, Father always remembered me and called me Susana. Relatives, friends, and neighbors wondered why he never forgot me no matter how long I stayed away from home. I, too, did not know why, but I always was very delighted to see Father stare at me for a minute, and before I even said anything or before I came close to him, he would call my name. Since my childhood, my siblings and my mother always said that I was my father's favorite child. If that was true, I thought that was why he never forgot me. It was only my mother and I whom Father never forgot.

It was always a joy to see him surrounded by his grandchildren, some combing his hair, others cutting his nails, while others asked him to give them goats to pay dowry for their dream wives. Now he was sick, and I knew he needed to go to a hospital immediately. I called my sisters, Mwende and Damaris, right away and asked them to take Dad to the hospital. After talking to them, a voice in my mind said, *Your father is so old. He is now sick, and you need to go home and see him. That is an emergency. Ask your sisters to ask the doctor who is going to treat him to write a report and fax it to you. Once you take that report to the immigration, you will be given advance parole to go and see your dad.* I did exactly that.

On the third day, I went to my computer to book an appointment for an interview at an immigration office. This time I tried very early in the morning, and by God's grace I thought, *If I cannot get an opening in Atlanta, I will try Memphis.*

Sure enough, I got an appointment in Memphis seven days before my travel date, but I wondered, *Where am I going to get the five working days that the immigration people told me?* Anyway, I was praying earnestly for God to work it out for me. I asked God to perform a miracle for me, because I knew that unless God worked out a way for me, I could not go on the trip, and I would lose the ticket money.

July 6, 2009, was the date of my interview in Memphis. I arrived in time. After showing my appointment letter and identification documents, I was directed to a window. The officer at this window told me to produce documents to show that I had an emergency that made it a necessity for me to get an advance parole in the shortest time possible. I gave him the doctor's letter stating that my father was more than one hundred years old and was sick. I, then, told him that I wanted to see my father while he was still alive. He told me to prove that that was my father. I gave him my birth certificate. After that the officer told me, "Sit there; I will give you the advance parole today. You will go home with it."

I did not know what to think of God. After about two hours, I was given the advance parole. David and our friend, Mr. Reggie, waited for me in the car. They did not know what to expect either. When I exited the building, they did not want to ask any questions. Instead, they focused their eyes on my face. My face told it all even before I opened my mouth. When I got back to school, my colleagues could not believe what had happened. A few days later, I left for Kenya where I had a wonderful time with my children, my father, and my other relatives.

However, that did not mark the end of my troubles. My R-1 visa was to expire in November, just three months from then. I did not have money to have it extended. Therefore, I started praying to God to perform another miracle for me to get my green card before the expiration date of my R-1 visa. Unfortunately, my friends told me to expect a delay with the green card application because I had interrupted the process by leaving the country. But I kept telling them that God would work it out for me. "I will pray to God to have the process move as if nothing happened," I told them.

God answered my prayers. On returning from Kenya, I found my green card in my mailbox. The processing of the document was not interrupted by my trip at all. If anything, the green card came earlier than I could ever have imagined. My colleagues, some of whom had applied for the same document long before I did, wanted to know whether I had used a very good lawyer. And I told them, "Yes, my lawyer, who is the Lord God of heaven, is a very good lawyer."

Of all my situations in life, my trip to Kenya and my green card demonstrated to me that God makes a way. Then I remembered some of my favorite verses in the Bible: "Be careful for nothing; but in every thing by prayer and supplication with thanksgiving let your requests be made known unto God. And the peace of God, which passeth all understanding, shall keep your hearts and minds through Christ Jesus" (Phil. 4:6, 7). "Therefore I say unto you, What soever ye desire, when ye pray, believe that ye receive them, and ye shall have them" (Mark 11:24).

Chapter 16

Missionary Work While in Kenya

The day that seemed as if it would never dawn came at last. It was time to go to Kenya to see my children and my parents. David had come to Advent Home to see me off. He took me to the Chattanooga airport where he caught a flight back to Houston as I took a shuttle to the Atlanta airport. From Atlanta I flew to the Netherlands and then to Nairobi, Kenya.

Throughout the many long hours of traveling, a few thoughts preoccupied my mind. *Are my children still holding on to God's ways, or have they gone astray? How do they take our separation now? Have they grown bitter about it, or do they still understand why I had to leave for the U.S.? What about my father? Will he still remember me when he sees me? What about my maternal grandmother? Can she still walk from her home to ours?*

I was not worried about my mother. She had only turned 70 in 2008. Compared to my father who was more than a hundred years old, she was too young for me to worry about her. In any case, her mother was still going strong. And my mother-in-law had come to the U.S. in July 2008, and I had spent time with her.

As I covered the many miles home, I was full of gratitude to God for all the miracles He had performed to make my stay in the U.S. tolerable and to make this trip a success. I remembered how I had received the money for my ticket and the advance parole. I also contemplated the success He had given me in teaching students with many dysfunctional behaviors. I knew I did not deserve all the grace and favors that God showed me. I kept thanking Him and praying for my trip to Kenya. I also prayed that my short trip would not get messed up by malaria. Throughout my life in Kenya, before I went to the

U.S., I often came down with malaria.

After about twenty-two hours of flying and waiting for connections in airports, I finally landed at Jomo Kenyatta International Airport on Tuesday evening. The only people who knew that I would be arriving on that day were my son and my friend Betty Muasya. Other friends and relatives knew I was coming home in July 2009, but they did not know the date or time. After I was told that I needed advance parole to travel, I told the few relatives who knew I was coming home that month that I was not sure whether I would make it at all. By the time I got the travel document, it was too late to make calls to Kenya and confirm that I was coming after all. The only time I had was for packing.

Furthermore, I did not want to tell many people the exact day and time of my arrival because I did not want them to come to the airport to wait for me. Why would I make a bunch of people come to the airport to wait for me at night! There was a terrible famine in Kenya at that time, and money was a big problem. I thought it would be better for my friends and relatives to spend their money on food and other necessities instead of spending it hiring cars to come and meet me at the airport. Whether they came to the airport or not, I was going to visit them in the villages and the towns where they lived. Well, the custom was just the opposite of what I did, and some people, especially my sisters, did not take it kindly. I apologized and explained myself, and I was forgiven.

Just the same, Wisdom and Betty met me at the airport. When Wisdom spotted me, he rushed toward me, stooped over, and clung to me. He had grown far taller than me. He had been taller than me when I left, but now he looked like a giant. Betty took me to her house in Lavington, Nairobi. After two days of contending with jetlag, I got ready to go visit my daughter in school. I arrived in Nairobi on Tuesday, and the following Sunday was a visiting day at her school. This is the time when parents cook all the delicacies they can afford and take them to school to eat with their children.

My daughter did not even know I was in Kenya. When I learned that I needed a travel document and that it was not easy to get , I had told her about my situation. She had cried one night and refused to be comforted at all. When I got the document at last, I decided to tell her about my visit when I was already in Nairobi. My son and I had planned to pay her a surprise visit, but my sister, Janiffer, spoiled our plan by telling Lulu that I was already in Nairobi and that I was going to visit her in school.

On that Sunday, Lulu stayed at a strategic place in school to make sure that she saw us when we appeared at the school gate. She knew Betty would drop Wisdom and I off, so she watched for Betty's car. When I exited the car near Lulu's dormitory, she tried to run but gave up because she was crying too much to run. We walked toward each other, and when we met, we embraced each other and remained in that position as Lulu continued to cry. It felt as if she would never let go. Finally, Betty left for a meeting; then the rest of us settled down to eat together and talk. "I told you that God would unite us again. He just did it," I reminded my children.

"Yeah, God is so good. Mommy, I can't believe I'm seeing you. Sometimes I used to think I would never see you again though we've always talked over the phone," Lulu said.

"All the time I waited for her at the airport, I felt like I was dreaming. When I hugged her, it became real," Wisdom said.

"I knew God would make it happen for us. You remember, I told you that before I left for the U.S. I have seen many people who have left children here and have gone for many, many years without coming back to see their children. I did not want that to happen to me, and I prayed to God to make it possible for me to come back soon to see you. And He did just that. God is so faithful; that's why I always tell you to trust Him," I told my children.

We ate the chapatti, stew, rice, vegetables, and fruits that Wisdom and I had prepared. Then we walked around the school compound talking and discussing the experiences of my children. They were very happy that I had come back to see them. On the other hand, they had many questions about the U.S. Soon it was 5:00 p.m., and it was time for all the visitors to leave the school compound. It would be another two weeks before schools would close for the August holidays, and Lulu would be allowed to come home to spend two weeks with me before I returned to the U.S. Lulu escorted us to the gate and went back to her dorm. This time she did not cry because she knew she was coming home to spend time with me.

Back in Lavington at Betty's house, I spent time with Wisdom in an effort to quietly find out whether my young son was still strong in the Lord. I was very glad that Wisdom was on a four-month break from the University of Nairobi. This gave me two weeks to concentrate on him before Lulu came. Pastor Randy Skeete from the U.S. was doing an evangelistic rally at the Lavington SDA Church in Nairobi. The rally was for all age groups starting from young children to adults. Wisdom was one of the teachers for the young children. The meetings for the young children started at 10:00 a.m. and ran until sometime in the evening. For the adults, the meetings started at 6:00 p.m. after people had left work. Betty's house, where my son and I stayed, was about three minutes' walk from the church. I got a chance to watch Wisdom teach the young children for several days.

Then, throughout the evenings, he would be busy helping Betty, who is the wife of the union president, organize stuff for the church. Later, I learned that he was having personal worship around 6:00 a.m. By the end of the second week of my stay in Nairobi, all of my fears about whether he was still holding on to the Lord had disappeared. I could not thank God enough for my son. Certainly, God had answered my prayer. Before I left Kenya for the U.S., I had prayed, "God, please let nothing take my children from Your mighty hands."

On Friday the following week, I decided to stop at Masii on my way to Makueni to see my parents. The Adventist school where I had worked before going to the U.S. was in that town. My sister-in-law, Alice, was the deputy principal by then. Wisdom and I stayed with Alice at her house so that on Sabbath we could go to the school's church together. I could not wait to see the whole school community.

All this time, I wanted to do some missionary work, but I did not know exactly what to do with so much limited time and almost no money. I prayed to God to tell me exactly what He wanted me to do because I knew the burden to do missionary work came from Him. Then a thought came to my mind. I remembered that at Masii Adventist School there were many needy students. A good number of them educated themselves through work programs.

I was impressed to ask Alice about the most needy students at that time.

"There is a student who was pierced by a thorn in his foot, and his whole foot has been swollen for weeks now. He went to the hospital, and he was told to go for an X-ray, but he does not have any money. That is the most needy case we have at the school right now," Alice told me.

"I will give you 1,000 Kenya shillings for him to go for the X-ray," I told her.

During my entire stay in the U.S., I always had a very heavy burden for Masii Adventist School. Sometimes I would cry for the school whenever I remembered that the students and staff worshipped under a big mango tree. During the dry season it was not a big problem, although for the times I preached under that mango tree church, I had to compete with the wind.

However, whenever it rained, it became too chaotic to hold a proper worship service. For the two years I had been in the U.S., I had prayed that God would open a way for me to help that school to get a building where they could hold worship on Sabbath without interruptions. It had not yet happened. Now here I was without enough money even to buy soap for the needy students. I wished I could help more students even if I could not help build a church for them.

On Sabbath morning, the 350 students and staff settled under the two adjacent mango trees that joined at the branches, giving them the appearance of just one humongous mango tree. The trees must have been planted in the '50s or early '60s. Those who planted them must have thought of the fruits that the trees would bear not knowing that they were building a church. The pulpit was prepared as usual: four or five chairs were arranged in front of the congregation. The staff sat around the students to keep an eye on every corner of the wide-open church. The students were excited to see me, especially those who were there before I left. I greeted them and promised to come visit with them when they were not in church. However, immediately after worship, the principal approached me and asked me whether I would talk to the students that Sabbath afternoon.

The only topic I thought about talking to the students was on God's faithfulness. At 2:00 p.m. the students and staff gathered under the two huge mango trees. After singing a few songs, the principal introduced me to the students and staff. "How many of you were students when I was here?" I asked them. All the form threes and fours raised their hands. Form threes and fours were there in form one and two by the time I left. "Those who were here, do you remember my favorite chorus?" I asked. Some put up their hands, and after some wrong answers, one student got it right.

"I will call upon the Lord," he said.

"Correct, that was my favorite chorus when I was here. Will you all help me sing it, please?" I requested. Under the mango trees, the high school boys and girls sang as the wind blew the voices across the village. We "called upon the Lord who is worthy to be praised." After singing I began my speech.

"I want to witness to you all that the Lord, God of heaven, is very faithful. And I am going to give you a summary of my experience with God right from the time I was a high school student like you up to this day. Before I tell you anything, I would like to know something. Does anybody here have any challenges in life? Do any of you have problems whether spiritual, academic, financial, social, or physical?"

Many hands went up. One by one I gave the students a chance to tell us their challenges. Some said that their parents did not have money and raising school fees was stressful for the whole family. Others said they had spiritual concerns because they did things they did not want to do. They wanted to do the right thing, but they always failed. Others said their grades in school were very bad, and they were very concerned about it.

"Okay, before we continue, how many of you believe what the Bible says is true?" I asked. Almost all hands went up. "For all those needs, whether financial, spiritual, or academic, I want you to know that I tested God with all of them, and I found Him faithful. I was born in a very poor family, and I went to a poor school like Masii Adventist School. I went to school at Mutitu SDA School. We had no library, and most of the textbooks we used as students we bought ourselves. My parents barely managed to pay the school fees for me. They could not afford to buy books for me. But I want you to know that, by God's grace, I never failed any exams then, whether internal or national. I borrowed books from students who came from rich homes. Some students had all the books, but they did not use them at all. That's why they gladly gave the books to me to read whenever I requested.

"Spiritually, I also had a huge problem. I had anger issues, and I used to fight both boys and girls. I had a terrible reputation in my village because of my fighting. The last time I fought was after completing high school. I fought a young man, and the whole village talked very poorly about me. They concluded by saying that I would never get a husband because I was fighting men. I did not like that. From that day on, I prayed to God to take away my anger and help me stop fighting forever. Since that day I have never fought again.

"Academically, I had a challenge too. When I first joined form one, I never used to do well in Bible. Also, throughout my life in high school, I never passed math. In form two, in K.J.S.E. exam I failed math. The only reason I passed the exam as a whole is that the examiners counted only six subjects. Therefore, out of eight subjects we only needed to pass in six subjects. In form four I again failed math, but I passed the whole exam with a division 2 because only six subjects were counted. Out of the eight that I sat for, I passed all but math.

"However, when I went to the university, I found out that I had to take math, and I had to pass it if I wanted to graduate. I feared registering for math for one year. Then, I realized there was no way I could avoid it. I prayed about it. Then I registered for math. By the end of the second week after registering, I noted the people who seemed to understand math very well. I approached them and suggested that we form a discussion group. They all agreed. We practiced math every day after class. At the end of the quarter, I earned a B in math.

"From that experience, I learned that my negative attitude toward math made me fail it. When I changed my attitude and practiced, I passed. Remember, 'I can do all things through Christ who strengthens me.' In addition, let nobody tell you that you are too foolish to learn. It is not true. Even if you make all F's in class, you are not stupid. You can learn. All you need is an extended time to study.

"In conclusion, I came from a family with abject poverty, but by God's grace I made it to university. And those who were here two years ago, I told you how God opened the way for me to go and teach in America. Coming straight from the village to go and teach in the U.S is something. And now in the U.S., the economy is very bad and people have been laid off from work. Eight workers were laid off from the organization for which I work, but I still have a job, by God's grace. If I tell you how God opened the way for me to come on this trip, you would be amazed. But all I can tell you in short is that God is very faithful. The Bible says, 'Ask and you will receive.' Trust in God and give Him all your problems or challenges, and He will work things out for you."

After Sabbath many students came to discuss with me different issues affecting them. At the end of the day, I forgot about the frustrated feeling I had the previous day because I did not have money to help many needy students.

Chapter 17

I Was Sent to Visit a Family

After spending the Sabbath day with students at Masii SDA School, I prepared to proceed to Makueni the following day to visit my parents. I bought a few presents for my dear parents. Then I left with my son and traveled to the village where I grew up. We arrived in the evening and found my father asleep. Mother and Martin, my nephew who is eight years old, were waiting for us. Mother could not believe that she was seeing me. We ate and talked until late at night when we finally went to sleep. By the time I woke up the next day, Mother was almost done milking the cows. I sat with her in the kitchen and helped prepare breakfast. Before we were even done with cooking porridge and a hot cocoa drink, Father woke up. He shuffled toward the kitchen, supporting himself with the wall of the house.

On seeing him, Mother shot up at once. She quickly went over to him, "Please wait there," she told him. Then she went inside the main house and brought out Father's walking stick. Father took the walking stick, but Mom still walked beside him toward the middle of the homestead between the kitchen and the main house. All this time I had been watching Father from the kitchen. I waited for him to settle down. After he was seated, I went out toward him but stopped three steps from him. He saw me and stopped looking around the homestead. He stared at me for a few seconds. Then Mother asked him, "Who is that?"

After about two seconds he said, "Susana." Both Mother and I could not believe it. Although he always called me by name, even after he had forgotten all of the other children, Mother and I did not expect him to remember me now, after staying in the U.S. for two years. After he recognized me, I went over to him and greeted him. He was so happy to see me. He also remembered that he had not seen me for a long time. "Where did you go?" he asked.

"I went to America," I said.

"How did you go there? It is so far away," he said.

"I used a plane," I said.

"Oh! You flew in the air, my child?" he asked.

"Yes, Father," I replied.

"How is your husband?" he inquired.

"He is well. He sent me to greet you and tell you that he loves you very much," I told him.

"I can see he is still taking good care of you," Father said.

"Yes, he is," I said.

Regardless of a woman's education or wealth, culture had it that a man had to ensure that his wife was well fed and well dressed. If she was sick, it was the man's responsibility to seek means for his wife to get proper treatment. To Father, I looked healthy and well dressed. That made him happy with my husband.

After talking with Father for some time, we ate breakfast. Mother and I had prepared cocoa and porridge. There were also loaves of bread and butter I had bought on my way home. After a short while, relatives and neighbors started coming home to greet me. As they came, the first person they saw outside was Father. So they would go straight to him and greet him very respectfully. If it was a man, Father would ask, "Whose son are you?" Then the person would shout into father's ear the name of his father. Father could see well, but he had lost his hearing. Father would remember the older generation of the village. The only problem was that all the men his age in the area had all passed away. He would ask whether the people he knew were doing well, but he was told they were dead. He would then become very quiet. I wondered what he was thinking.

Then I asked him, "Father do you remember when you were a watchman in Nairobi and a lot of your colleagues and friends were killed by thugs and others by lions?"

"Yes, I remember. God has been very good to me. I did not know I would retire from being a watchman and come home to live and grow this old. Yet, all my friends, even those who stayed at the village, are dead," he said.

"Yes, Father, God is very good. He answered your prayers. You always prayed for His care and protection," I said. It was a delight to see my father again. Even the villagers seemed pleased to talk to him. Everyone respected Father not only because of his old age but because of the kind of person he was. Before he went to Nairobi, he was the headman of the village. He settled all the cases in the village. When he came back to the village, before he grew so old, the villagers made him the headman again. And Father had wisdom to deal with everybody respectfully but also firmly.

I thanked God so much for making it possible to see my father again. We spent the day talking and cooking with my mother and receiving visitors who brought me so many live chickens to eat. They did not know I had embraced a vegan diet since going to Advent Home. All the same, I received the chickens and thanked them very much.

On the second day at home, I woke up early in the morning, and instead of staying in bed to contemplate what I would do for my morning worship, I was impressed to go for a walk in the village. My mind told me to take 200 Kenya shillings with me and go to visit a particular family in the village. I prayed about the impressions and then took the 200 shillings and left. Since it was so early in the morning, I decided to take the main road instead of going through the bushes. It took me about twenty minutes to reach the home I was impressed to visit. The homestead did not have a sign of anybody awake.

"Anybody home," I called. There was silence.

"Anybody home," I called again. Then I stood outside one of the huts. As I stood there, a young man, around fifteen years old, came out.

"Oh! Did I wake you up?" I asked.

"Not really. I was not asleep," he said.

"How is everybody in this family?" I asked.

"We are alright," he replied.

"Where is your mom?" I asked.

"She is at the farm," he said as he pointed in the direction where his mother was.

"Thank you very much. Let me go and see her," I said as I left for the farm. *It is so early in the morning, and there is nothing in the farms. What is she doing in the garden?* After a few steps in the direction the young man had pointed me to, I saw his mother walking slowly from one pigeon peas tree to another. "Mother," I called a few steps away. She turned and saw me.

"Ah, Susana, where have you come from?" She was surprised to see me.

"I have come from home," I told her.

"When did you come from America?" she asked.

"I came last week. What are you doing in the garden?" I asked.

"Well, I just came to see whether I could get a few seeds of peas," she said.

After the formal greetings, she took me home and brought a three-legged stool for me. She too brought hers from one of the huts and sat next to me. As we continued talking, her husband came from one of the huts and greeted me very warmly; he then joined us.

After talking for some time and asking how everybody was doing in the family, she told me, "Susana, I cannot give you anything to eat. We have not had real food in this home for three days. It has been very hard for us because our son who used to help us lost his job in Nairobi. For months now he has been looking for a job, but he hasn't found one yet. The cows we would have sold died because of the drought. Now we are waiting on God to provide for us."

"Don't worry about me. I'm all right, and I am so sorry to hear about all that, but I'm glad you trust God to provide for you. God is so faithful, and when we put all our trust in Him, He never disappoints us. Can we pray together?" I requested.

"Yes, let us pray," she said.

I prayed and then I gave her the 200 shillings and invited her, her husband, and her son to come to my mother's home for lunch. Unfortunately, the mother and son could not come. Her leg was hurt, and she could not walk to my mother's home. And the boy had to be sent somewhere. Her husband promised to come on behalf of the family.

"Oh, I wish I had a car to come for you, but I don't. My brother-in-law, Elisha, dropped me at home, and he will come for me when the time comes for me to go back to Nairobi," I told her.

"Don't worry, Susana. You have already done so much for us. God must have sent you. I don't know what we would have done today," she said.

I Was Sent to Visit a Family

Although I did not have a lot of money to give them, I thanked God so much that He had sent me to the family to give them something at least for that day. When I reached home, I told my mother that at lunchtime, I would have a special visitor so I was going to do some of the cooking. I cooked chapatti, stew, and cabbage. I was glad that I bought some food on my way to Mom's home.

The man came and ate lunch with us. Then I asked him whether he could carry some food for his wife and son. He accepted. I packed food for his family. Later, I thought about the whole episode and got so excited about how God had used me to help a family even though I felt that I did not have money and that I could not do much. I learned that I do not need to have thousands or millions of dollars to do God's work. There is so much to be done with the little that I have right now.

Chapter 18

Back to the U.S. With Anxiety

"That is a very wealthy member of parliament in Kenya. Why is he weeping?" I asked.

"The rich also cry," a calm small voice told me. Then I woke up. It was 1:00 a.m. I stayed awake for some time, asking myself the meaning of this dream.

"The poor and the rich all have problems. Do not focus so much on asking God to give you financial freedom, thinking that once you get it you will find peace and joy. Real peace and joy come from God alone. 'You will keep in perfect peace, whose mind is stayed on you: because he trusts in you,' (Isa. 26:3)," The calm small voice told me.

After spending two years at Advent Home, I thought I had learned to totally surrender my life into God's hands and follow His guidance in all my endeavors. But this was early October 2009, and since mid-August I had been praying to God to give me guidance on how to continue writing this book. By this time, I was used to praying and asking Him what He wanted me to put down, and ideas seemed to just flow. But for nearly two months now, I had not written one sentence. I prayed every day, but nothing came. I started thinking I had committed some sin that made God too angry to speak to me.

I repented of both known and unknown sins. But days turned into weeks. I could not hear the voice of God giving me instructions on what to write. I became anxious and worried. For some time I did not know what to say in prayer. However, I continued praying, but no inspiration came. I knew something was wrong, but I did not understand what it was. I became stressed.

One evening I went to bed and switched off the lights to sleep, but I couldn't fall asleep. I was in agony. I felt the pain of being separated from God. Then I cried, "Lord, I surrender to you totally. I cannot fear and run away from You. I have nowhere to go. Even if I have to die, I will die in Your hands. I know You, Father. You are loving, kind, just, and faithful. That's why for the remaining days of my life, I will worship You and do Your will by Your own grace. Help me to read Your Word and wait upon You. Even if I never hear Your voice the way I want to, give me grace to still trust You. In Jesus' name I pray. Amen."

Immediately after finishing this prayer, I sensed instant light in my bedroom. Although my eyes were closed and full of tears and the lights were off, I felt as if somebody had flashed light in the room. I sensed peace and calmness. Then I immediately fell asleep. The next day my cell phone alarm went off at 5:00 a.m. I turned it off and reset it to 6:00 a.m. I stayed in bed but did not fall asleep again. Then the calm voice that had told me that the rich also cry spoke to me.

"You have been in such a rush and deep anxiety to hear the voice of God. You have prayed and cried, asking why God has been silent and not speaking to you to give you instructions. But you could not hear His voice in that rush, anxiety, and worry. You need to be still to hear the voice of God," the calm voice said.

"Oh, God, please forgive me. I thought I had learned to trust You with my problems and my needs. Here I am again, Lord. I have failed. Please forgive me and continue to teach me how to pray and wait patiently upon You, Father," I prayed.

At this point, I remembered how, since I had returned to the U.S. on August 19, 2009, from visiting Kenya, I had been concerned about many things. First, my children attended boarding schools in Nairobi. Therefore, while I was visiting them, I had needed to be in the city so that I could easily see my daughter at Kenya High and keep company with my son who was at the University of Nairobi. Because of our constant need to be in the city of Nairobi, I had strongly felt that we needed to have a place of our own there. However, I did not even have the money to stay in a hotel with my children. Fortunately, Pastor Stephen Muasya, the then president of the East African Union and his wife, Betty, were very kind to us. They welcomed us into their house in Lavington whenever we were in Nairobi.

Secondly, I had always wanted to help the poor, especially young people. Now that I had just come from Kenya, my burden had increased. I had seen so many people who needed help. My heart was touched by so many situations, yet I could do nothing because I had no money. Masii Adventist School was still worshipping under the two huge mango trees. Countless people were hungry and in need of clothing. I came back from Kenya very frustrated.

Finally, when I arrived back in the U.S., I realized that I had not kept track of the exchange rate between the U.S. dollar and the Kenyan shilling. As a result, I had overdrawn my account in the U.S. by almost $400. Every time I had withdrawn money, I had written down what I thought was the balance of my account in the U.S., so I did not understand where I had gone wrong in my accounting. The ATM machines I used in Kenya did not show me the balance of my account.

In addition, by this time, our ministry at Advent Home was not doing well financially; therefore, the administration cut the employees' salaries by 25 percent. With all of my bills and obligations to help family and other people in need, I did not know how to pay for the $400 overdraft.

In spite of this pathetic financial situation, I needed to start processing green cards for my children before it was too late. This meant paying thousands of dollars to my lawyer and to the USCIS. *With a salary of less than a thousand dollars a month, $400 bank overdraft, and bills because of my trip, where am I going to start?* I wondered. *When will I ever save the money needed to pay my lawyer?*

To make matters worse, while in Kenya I discovered that my car had broken down and my son had taken it to a mechanic to fix. The mechanic claimed to have spent 20,000 shillings on it, which I needed to pay him before he would release the car to my son. I did not have the money.

Furthermore, I had left a Nissan matatu, a fourteen-passenger van for public transport, in Nairobi under the supervision of my sister, but she had mismanaged the business. While in Africa, I could not afford a rental car, so my children and I had to use public transport or go on foot whenever we could. By the time I came back to the U.S., I had deep cuts on the soles of my feet from walking on dusty roads. I came back to the U.S. thinking about each of these situations and wondering where to start in fixing all of them. Without knowing, I had succumbed to self-pity, anxiety, and worry.

Back at Advent Home, I resumed working, but my mind was always on the people I had seen with so many needs, especially children whose parents had died from AIDS. Many of these children had dropped out of school for a lack of money to pay school fees. I kept trying to think of ways I could help, but I could not come up with anything even though I felt that I should be in a position to help. In addition, my extended family needed help too. With all this in mind, I lost focus. Instead of seeing a bigger God than all the needs, I focused on the needs and slowly started to pity myself. I earnestly prayed to God, but I did not realize that I was rushing Him to fix all these problems quickly. God was talking to me, as I came to learn later, but I could not hear His voice. I got myself so mixed up that I could not think straight and concentrate in writing this book.

It was in this messed up situation that I forgot Philippians 4:6, 7: "Be careful for nothing; but in every thing by prayer and supplication with thanksgiving let your requests be made known to God. And the peace of God, which passeth all understanding, shall keep your hearts and minds through Christ Jesus."

After the small calm voice told me to be still so as to hear the voice of God, I understood afresh Matthew 6:25-34. I saw the love of God for us when He told us not to worry about what we should eat or drink or what we shall put on. God knows if we get worried we will only make our situation worse and will not be in a position to let Him help us with our problems. Our minds and hearts will be too crowded by worries to hear the Lord directing us out of our messed up situations. *Will I ever became mature enough to not worry when I am faced with too heavy a problem? Oh God, please increase my faith and trust in You.*

Then I remembered Ellen White's writing, "We are so anxious, all of us, for happiness, but many rarely find it because of their faulty method of seeking, in the place of striving" (*Mind, Character, and Personality*, vol. 2. p. 472). I prayed for God's grace to do as instructed in Matthew 6:33: "But seek ye first the kingdom of God, and his righteousness; and all these things shall be added unto you." After this, I was able to continue writing this book.

"Putting our trust in God, we are to move steadily forward, doing His work with unselfishness, in humble dependence upon Him, committing ourselves and our present and future to His wise providence, holding the beginning of our confidence firm unto the end, remembering that it is not because of our worthiness that we receive the blessings of heaven, but because of the worthiness of Christ, and our acceptance, through faith in Him, of God's abounding grace" (Ellen G. White, *Testimonies for the Church*, vol. 9, p. 29).

Chapter 19

Distracted From Writing

After writing fourteen chapters of this book, I wanted to end it there. But I was impressed to keep on writing more chapters. Unfortunately, at this point, the enemy stood firmly determined that this book would never be completed. For six months, I was totally unable to write anything or to review the completed chapters. Yet to complete this project and move on to other endeavors was one of the deepest desires of my heart. Unfortunately, during this time, I was totally unable to do anything to accomplish my goal.

This situation began with distractions that came from all corners of my life. However, when the distractions started, I did not recognize them as such. At first I thought I just had many things that required my attention. I could not write then because I spent my time on those other matters. In addition, most of the issues that took up my time involved friends, colleagues, or relatives. Sometimes it was socializing with friends. Other times it was dealing with issues, both pleasant and disappointing, that seemed to come up so often. For example, at one time key colleagues became hostile for no apparent reason. One person started spreading rumors about me. At home, things were no better. Some relatives in my extended family stopped talking to me. Whenever I asked them what the problem was, they just said, "Nothing."

I decided to talk to the people involved in mistreating me and find out what the problem was. I talked to the woman involved in spreading rumors about me and those who deliberately mistreated me. My interest was to find out what I was doing to provoke them. I wanted to know what I needed to do differently. However, none of my accusers were interested in talking honestly or solving the problems. Just the same, I told them I did not appreciate what they were doing to me.

Every time I wanted to write, somebody would seek to talk to me or need me to do something urgent. However, the worst distractions were my thoughts. Whenever I was awake, I had something on my mind. All the time, I felt as if there were people arguing or narrating endless stories to me. Most of the time, it would be rewinding something that happened or thinking about something I wanted to do. My mind was perpetually occupied by different types of thoughts, going over and over certain thoughts for hours until it went to something else.

This was a very frightening experience for me. I prayed to get my mind focused on God and this project that He had given me to do. I also prayed for peace and calmness, but my mind kept worrying. This caused severe anxiety and temptations, yet I had no control. As a result, I was not calm enough to concentrate on writing. Whenever the thought of writing came to my mind, I went blank. Even when I knew what to write, my mind could not construct the sentences.

At first I thought I was just having writer's block, combined with many problems, until one night I had a dream. In the dream, I was sent to attend to a sick person. I meant to go, but I did not know that I was walking in the opposite direction of the person's home. After going for about five miles, I started wondering why I was not reaching the home. I asked a woman I met on the way whether she knew the home of the sick person. She told me that I was going in the opposite direction. Immediately, a voice in the dream told me, "You are wasting time." Then I woke up.

Upon waking up, I remembered I had not worked on my book for at least four weeks. I started reviewing my activities for those weeks to find out how I had spent my time apart from my working hours. I realized that I had been chasing the wind. From that day on, I decided to give all the rumors and accusations against me to God and move on. Also, I limited the time I spent talking and socializing with my family and friends. I also decided that the time I set aside for writing would not be spent on anything else unless there was an emergency. However, even after determining that I would resume writing, I still could not do it because my thoughts were not organized.

After a few months stuck in this situation, I realized that something was really wrong. But I did not know what. Just the same, I also decided never to

Distracted From Writing

give up. I kept praying about it and reading Bible verses such as Isaiah 26:3: "Thou wilt keep him in perfect peace, whose mind is stayed on thee: because he trusteth in thee." I kept pleading with God to keep my mind fixed on Him. That would happen for a short time, and then my mind would start wandering again.

I intensified my reading of the Bible and other religious books to find out what was happening to me. I read, "For thousands of years Satan has been experimenting upon the properties of the human mind, and he has learned to know it well. By his subtle workings in these last days he is linking the human mind with his own, imbuing it with his thoughts; and he is doing this work in so deceptive a manner that those who accept his guidance know not that they are being led by him at his will" (Ellen G. White, *Mind, Character, and Personality*, vol. 1, p. 18). Now I knew Satan was behind the confusion I felt in my mind. And things got worse whenever I prayed about writing this book. After some time, I realized the enemy was blocking my writing. Then I started praying to God to overcome this battle for me.

Furthermore, to help myself overcome the trials, I read stories such as the one about Nehemiah when he was building the wall of Jerusalem. Each time his enemies sent for him to distract him from building, he replied, "I am doing a great work, so that I cannot come down: why should the work cease, whilst I leave it, and come down to you? Yet they sent unto me four times after this sort; and I answered them after the same manner" (Neh. 6:3, 4).

Whenever I compared myself to Nehemiah, I found myself guilty of entertaining people who were deliberately set to distract me. I also considered the way Jesus dealt with Satan when the devil tempted Him. "It is written" Jesus told him every time. Eventually, Jesus told him, "Get thee hence, Satan: for it is written, Thou shalt worship the Lord thy God, and him only shalt thou serve. Then the devil leaveth him, and, behold, angels came and ministered unto him" (Matt. 4:10, 11). Jesus did not give Satan a chance to distract Him. The Savior was forthright with the devil.

If I had been like Jesus right from the start, maybe Satan would not be so adamant, I thought. Countless times I repented and asked God to cleanse me from all unrighteousness and overcome Satan for me.

Then, I was impressed to read *Mind, Character, and Personality*: "Cast out of heaven, Satan set up his kingdom in this world, and ever since he has been untiringly striving to seduce human beings from their allegiance to God. He uses the same power that he used in heaven—the influence of mind on mind. Men become tempters of their fellowmen" (vol. 1, p. 28).

That was exactly what was happening to me. By then I knew the people Satan was using to either distract or frustrate me. And many times, I wondered whether these people knew what they were doing or whether the enemy was using them without their knowledge.

Anyway, I realized that these brothers and sisters were not the enemy. Therefore, I prayed, "God, I choose to forgive these people. Please give me grace to love them and treat them well." By God's grace I remained loving and caring, and whenever they came to me with their suggestions or did things to frustrate me, I took the opportunity to teach them Bible principles. At first it never seemed to help them at all. But I kept praying and reading the Bible and other books so as to remain focused on my mission. I also prayed for each of these people for God's Spirit to prevail upon them and lead them to repentance. But I also decided to stay away from those I knew were out to distract me. I decided not to expose myself unnecessarily to trials and temptations anymore.

Then one morning the Spirit of the Lord directed me to read *The Great Controversy*. As I went over the table of contents, my attention was drawn to two chapters: "Agency of Evil Spirit" and "Snares of Satan." After reading the two chapters, I understood the message God was communicating to me. I realized that I was in the middle of a fierce battle. I learned practically that "the followers of Christ know little of the plots which Satan and his hosts are forming against them.… The Lord permits His people to be subjected to the fiery ordeal of temptation, not because He takes pleasure in their distress and affliction, but because this process is essential to their final victory. He could not, consistently with His glory, shield them from temptation, for the very object of the trial is to prepare them to resist all the allurements of evil" (p. 528).

I understood the message. I knew God had allowed Satan to tempt me and that Satan was blocking me from completing the book. I told the Lord, "Father, it has been months now. Please let these trials and temptations go away from me. Lord, your Word says, 'But God is faithful, who will not allow you to be tempted above that ye are able; but will with the temptation also make a way to escape, that ye may be able to bear it' (1 Cor. 10:13)."

Unfortunately, the confusion in my mind would not clear. I could not think of what to write, and I did not have the strength or peace I needed to review the completed chapters. For six months I could not feel the presence of God the way I was used to. Many times He answered my prayers, but not about writing this book or clearing my mind from the confusion that existed. I prayed very hard to hear His voice clearly guiding me, but He was quiet.

In addition to the silence that I felt existed between God and me, and besides the confusion in my mind, my body suffered from serious fatigue. All the time, I was either in pain or too tired to sit next to a computer and type. Other times, I instantly became too sleepy to stare at the computer screen. Well, I knew all this was the doing of the enemy, so I kept praying to God to overcome this battle for me. By then I could not even remember the flow of my writing. It had been many months since I had written or even read what I had written. Now I knew it would take only the mighty hand of God for me to resume writing.

Although I did not give up, I reached a point when I ceased to understand why God was taking so long to help me overcome. At times I wondered whether I had done something that made Him give up on me. But the Bible says, "If we confess our sins, he is faithful and just to forgive us our sins, and to cleanse us from all unrighteousness" (1 John 1:9). I reminded God about this verse countless times.

I reached a point where I did not see any end to my suffering. Then I told God, "Lord, I really do not understand what is happening anymore. However, I will continue trusting and loving You, my God and my Redeemer." I decided not to be stressed about the silence anymore. But I decided to pray and wait, even if it took the remaining days of my life.

"Let us hold fast the profession of our faith without wavering; (for he is faithful that promised)" (Heb. 10:23). This verse encouraged me many times. I chose to hang on to faith alone because there was nothing in sight. *When soldiers go to war, they fight until they win the war or until they are killed by the enemy. If people fight so relentlessly for earthly countries, how much more should we fight for our heavenly country?* This thought encouraged me.

The good thing about this war between good and evil is that Jesus won the war already, both in heaven and on earth. In addition, we know the end result of this war. These thoughts kept me going. I knew God was speaking to me to hold on to my faith. Although I could not powerfully feel His presence around me or hear His voice as clearly as I always did, deep down in my heart I believed that God was keenly watching over me. I knew every encouraging thought came from Him. However, because I felt His presence so faintly, I experienced the pain of prolonged loneliness and the confusion of delayed promises. At that time, I came to appreciate Bible warnings such as, "Be sober, be vigilant; because your adversary the devil, as a roaring lion, walketh about, seeking whom he may devour" (1 Pet. 5:8).

From my experience I learned that God never gives up on us. Satan never gives up either. Therefore, I knew, if I chose to give up, the battle between good and evil would still continue, but I would give up on life. By God's grace I chose to wait on the Lord. I constantly prayed for my faith to hold.

Then I waited upon the Lord to deliver me.

Chapter 20

God Overcame for Me

"For more than twenty years since we started practicing in our law firm, we have never seen anything like this. How could the U.S. Embassy in Nairobi call your children for an interview before we gave them all the documents they needed? We have not even paid for their interview. You must be using another lawyer," my attorney's legal assistant told me over the phone.

"The only other lawyer I am using is God. I have no money to pay two lawyers," I responded.

"Susan, are you sure your husband has not used another lawyer to handle the immigration case of your children?"

This was the third or fourth time she had asked me this question, and I had given her the same answer. "I am sure. You sound so flabbergasted by this case. Please call the USCIS and ask them what happened. They will tell you." I told her.

Ten minutes later she called me and told me, "I called the USCIS to inquire about the case of your children, and they told me that your son was aging out. That's why the USCIS expedited the cases."

In January 2010 I called my lawyer and told him that I wanted to start processing green cards for my children. In our conversation, I told him that my son was turning twenty-one on May 29, 2010. Then my lawyer told me that I had to move fast, otherwise, my son would age out, and I would not be able to process the document for him. Moving fast meant paying money both to my lawyer and the USCIS. I did not have the money. That is why I had delayed starting the process. I prayed about it and went to talk to my director to give me a loan. By God's grace the director authorized it, and I was given the money I needed to start the process. By the time I paid the money to my lawyer, it was February. My lawyer told me that the case would take about six months for it to be approved. If it took six months my son would be cut out by age.

I went to God in prayer and told Him, "Lord, there aren't six months between February and May, and I really want my children to get green cards so that they can come here and be with me. God of heaven, you know one of the desires of my heart is to see my family reunited. I don't know what you are going to do, but I am asking you to organize this case so that by the end of May the final stage of this case will be approved. This is beyond me, but I know that nothing puzzles You, God of heaven. But let Your will be done. In Jesus' name I pray. Amen." I did the paperwork and waited.

About two months later, I received letters from the USCIS telling me that the two cases were approved. This was the first stage. Then my lawyer asked for more money to pay for the final stage of the cases. Again, God provided the money, and I sent it to my lawyer for his legal fees and for the USCIS. Then my lawyer sent me more documents to fill out. In addition, he asked for passport-sized photos of the children, medical examination reports, and police documents to clear the children of any criminal records. It was during the time they were collecting these documents that my son called and told me that the U.S. Embassy in Nairobi had sent him and his sister a lot of documents to fill out and had scheduled an interview for May 27, 2010.

I told him to forward the documents to me; then I passed them on to my lawyer. Everybody in the law firm got perturbed because they were waiting for me to send them all the documents so that they could forward them to USCIS and pay for the interviews. After all this, a report would be sent to the U.S. Embassy in Nairobi so that they could call the children for interviews. This was the third week of May. There was one week remaining, and my son would be cut off by age. In addition, it would take more time for the documents to reach my lawyer in Atlanta, and then send the same to the USCIS and back to Nairobi. There was no time for all that.

God intervened and saw to it that the cases were expedited, and the children were scheduled for interviews on May 27, 2010, two days before my son's birthday. What my lawyer could not understand was who argued in favor of the children so that they could be called to the U.S. Embassy in Nairobi for interviews before all the documents had been sent to the USCIS and before the money had been paid for the interview. I knew God had done it. While my lawyer was panicking, the children were very peaceful. The consulate at the U.S. Embassy in Nairobi had sent them all the forms they needed to fill out and instructed the children on what to carry with them on the day of the interview. And two days before my son exceeded the eligible age, both children were given visas to come to the U.S. for their green cards.

This was the second time my lawyer was taken aback by my case. I wrote him a detailed e-mail and told him, "Sir, as I told you before, I did not use any other lawyer. However, I gave the cases of my children to God to organize and see to it that my son met the age limit. God answered my prayer once again. That is why it went the way it did. I was not surprised at all because that is what I asked God to do. The God of heaven is very faithful. That's why I trust Him."

While my lawyer and his team were surprised by these cases, I was not. Just before the U.S. Embassy in Nairobi called the children for their interviews, the Holy Spirit told me to fast and pray for the immigration cases of my children. I did. Then I waited on God to do His will.

When the Holy Spirit instructed me to fast and pray for my children, it was the first time I heard God's voice so clearly in six months. This incident reopened free communication between me and God. The silence that had existed for six long months came to an end just before the end of May. God spoke to me and assured me of fulfilling His promises to me. One of the promises was to lead me to finish writing this book and to get it published so that it could be distributed around the world as a witness for Him. The Holy Spirit resumed His guidance in my writing.

However, though I resumed writing, I kept wondering what exactly had happened in the last six months when I was not able to write anything. Then one night I had a dream. In the dream I saw myself standing in a line to enter an office where I needed very important urgent service. The line moved fast, and soon there were only two people before it would be my turn. At that point, I decided to step out of the line for a few minutes.

When I got out of the line, my attention was caught by a group of people who looked like skeletons. Yet, they were talking and drinking. I stood there looking at them. They stared at me and started whispering to each other. One of them said, "She looks brave." Then I felt strange around them, and I decided to go back to the line. To my surprise, all the people had been served and the office was closed. I stood at the door wondering what to do. Then one of the officers who had been serving people came over to me and got ready to reopen the office and serve me. Unfortunately, I realized that when I stepped out of line and walked away from the office, I lost the documents I needed to present in the office in order to be served. The officer told me to get my documents together and go back.

I woke up in deep remorse because I instantly understood the meaning of the dream. I realized I ceased writing for six months because I shifted my attention from the book to other activities that held me. By the time I realized what was happening, I had lost the focus and the concentration I needed to write. Furthermore, my mind got too crowded to clearly hear God's voice. Then I got into a similar predicament to the one of Mary and Joseph. "And when they had fulfilled the days, as they returned, the child Jesus tarried behind in Jerusalem; and Joseph and his mother knew not of it. But they, supposing him to have been in the company, went a day's journey; and they sought him among their kinsfolk and acquaintances. And when they found him not, they turned back again to Jerusalem, seeking him. And it came to pass, that after three days they found him in the temple" (Luke 2:43-46).

It took Mary and Joseph three days to find Jesus after traveling without him for one day. For a full day they thought they had Jesus in their company. I do not know how many days it took me to lose my focus of writing this book, but I know it took me six months to get back on track.

Looking back at the six months of my trials and temptations, I thank God for the lessons I learned. Yes, it was painful when I went through it, but I learned lessons I could not have learned otherwise. Now I understand the controversy between God and Satan better. The situation made me read books I had never read in my Christian life. After resisting trials and temptations for six long months, by God's grace I am wiser and stronger in Christ. God provided the power to overcome.

I have no words to describe God's mercy and love for His people. In addition, I learned through experience that the only way for me to overcome trials and temptations and remain focused on my mission as a Christian is to live on my knees, to surrender as many times a day as I can. Also, I learned that God was always ready for me. I was the one who walked away and got distracted. Therefore, I was the one who needed to get back to where I was supposed to be.

Furthermore, I realized that, "Neither wicked men nor devils can hinder the work of God, or shut out His presence from His people, if they will, with subdued, contrite hearts, confess and put away their sins, and in faith claim His promises. Every temptation, every opposing influence, whether open or secret, may be successfully resisted" (*The Great Controversy,* p. 529). Also, "Not by might, nor by power, but by my spirit, saith the LORD of hosts" (Zech. 4:6).

Always being aware of the enemy who did not want me to complete this project, I surrendered to God every day. I constantly asked God "not to lead me into temptation but to deliver me from evil."

Then I remembered Jesus telling His disciples, "This kind can come forth by nothing, but by prayer and fasting" (Mark 9:29). I decided to fast and pray until I completed writing this book. Before, I had tried to avoid eating supper in order to lose some weight, but I was not successful. In the evenings I felt too hungry to avoid supper. But this time I asked God to enable me. As I write this chapter, I am fasting for the second week in a row, and I believe I will be able to go on until I complete the project.

In addition, I needed peace of mind and also to keep my mind fixed on God's will for me. So I kept reading His word: "Above all, taking the shield of faith, wherewith ye shall be able to quench all the fiery darts of the wicked. And take the helmet of salvation, and the sword of Spirit, which is the word of God: Praying always with all prayers and supplication in the Spirit, and watching thereunto with all perseverance and supplication for all saints" (Eph. 6:16-18).

I found God incredibly loving, caring, and faithful. To me, He fulfilled His promise that "Thou wilt keep him in perfect peace, whose mind is stayed on thee: because he trusteth in thee" (Isa. 26:3). God cleared my mind completely. The confusion I felt in my head and the fatigue I felt before disappeared. Also, the perpetual drama of distractions that streamed from friends, colleagues, and relatives came to an end. When God came on stage, all the other channels were dismantled. But I knew the enemy would not leave me alone forever.

Therefore, I prayed for strength of spirit, mind, and body. God answered my prayers. After leaving the office at six, I would exercise, take a shower, have worship, and write until 10:00 p.m. Then I would sleep until five in the morning when I would wake up and have worship and write again until 7:30 a.m. Amazingly, I felt strong and alert. I knew this was God's grace because before I felt too tired to write either after six or early in the morning. The body aches, sleep, and the confusion in my head that dominated me so much during the time of my trials disappeared.

Speaking from experience, I know there is victory in Jesus. I have come to trust God totally, and I know whatever He promises to do in the future He will do because whatever He promised to do in the past He did.

This hope makes me very excited, especially when I see all the promises God has given us in the Bible. "For the LORD God is a sun and shield: the LORD will give grace and glory: no good thing will he withhold from them that walk uprightly" (Ps. 84:11).

"Delight thyself also in the LORD: and he shall give thee the desires of thine heart. Commit thy way unto the LORD; trust also in him; and he shall bring it to pass" (Ps. 37:4, 5).

"Therefore I say unto you, What soever ye desire, when ye pray, believe that ye receive them, and ye shall have them" (Mark 11:24).

This book cannot contain all God's promises to us, but I will emphasize that I have found God incredibly loving, caring, and faithful. I have found Him worthy of my trust because His promises are true. I have learned not to worry about anything I have put in His hands because He organizes my business much better than I can. I confirmed that God will never abandon me or let Satan try me beyond what I can take.

Chapter 21

I Received a Call

It was 6:00 a.m. when the phone rang in my bedroom. I answered it, wondering who was calling me that early in the morning. It was one of my prayer partners and a spiritual mentor at Advent Home.

"Hello! Good morning," she greeted me.

"Good morning, Mom," I responded.

"How are you doing?" she asked.

"I'm doing well. I thank God," I told her.

"Tell me, are you leaving?" she inquired.

"Do you mean leaving Advent Home?" I asked.

"Yes," she said.

"I'm planning to in a month's time," I said.

"Listen, I just finished doing my morning worship. Then I picked the phone to call a certain woman at Wildwood. Immediately after lifting the phone, I was told, 'Call Susan.' I said, 'I am not calling Susan. I am calling this woman at Wildwood.' The voice said, 'Call Susan; she is leaving.' Then I called you at once. So what's happening?" she asked.

"It is just as I told you a month ago. After I finish my contract with Advent Home, I would like to go to Texas and join my husband. Remember, we prayed about it to seek God's will," I told her.

"When does your contract with Advent Home end?" she asked.

"July 6, but I gave my notice to leave by the end of August," I responded.

"Have you found another job in Texas, or what are your plans?" she asked.

"No. Not yet," I told her

"Okay, dear, the Lord has just confirmed it. You are leaving," she said.

"I thank God for speaking at last. Now I will move with confidence," I said.

This was the beginning of July 2010. I had been at Advent Home for three years. Before I came to the U.S., I had promised to teach for Advent Home for three years. That is why Advent Home sent a petition letter to the U.S. Embassy in Nairobi asking them to give me a visa to go and teach for them for three years. Because the American Embassy in Nairobi was convinced that Advent Home needed me, they gave me the visa. As much as possible, I always want to keep my word.

By the end of the three years, I had become good at my job, and I liked it. In addition, new students came to Advent Home throughout the year. Every time a new student came, I saw a deeper need and it confirmed why I needed to be at this special school to help the new students.

However, by the end of the three years, a very deep longing had surfaced in my heart to join David in Texas. All the same, I did not want to leave unless God assured me that it was in His perfect will for me to go. Since Advent Home was my wilderness, I had determined in my heart that I would never leave until God assured me that I was done with my training. Every day I prayed to God to give me the patience and perseverance I needed to keep my promise to Advent Home and to go through my training according to His will. This is why the call from my prayer partner was very important to me. In fact, I did not feel at peace to look for a job in Texas before I knew that God had blessed my plans to leave my wilderness.

Now that I was comfortable with leaving, I talked about it freely with my colleagues and friends. Then the chaplain asked me whether I would like to conduct morning worship for the students before I left. Leading students in worship was my favorite duty at Advent Home. The chaplain gave me a Friday morning. In our worship we talked about "The Power in the Blood of Jesus." Then after worship I told the students, "Good people, guess what! Ms. Susan is graduating from Advent Home." All the students clapped for me, but the older students clapped louder and for a longer time. The older students understood what it meant to graduate from Advent Home. New students did not understand fully how the system worked.

This was mid-August and almost half of the students were new. They had to learn that for them to graduate from Advent Home they had to earn three hundred and fifty points. These points came from evaluations that were based on seventy objectives touching on all aspects of growth: spiritual, mental, social, and physical. Resident care staff, teachers, and work industry staff all evaluated students at different times and awarded them points according to their conduct in all the areas. Every time a student fought or ran away from school, he lost some points. When a student obeyed and followed instructions consistently for a week, he earned points.

Therefore, for a student to graduate, he had to overcome defiance, cursing, fighting, and refusing to do school work and many other dysfunctional behavioral issues. It took a lot of guidance, counseling, teaching, and undoing of bad habits. For some students it took months. For others, it took years, and it all depended on how deep the dysfunctional behaviors were and how much cooperation a student gave to the staff so that he could learn.

In our worship that Friday morning, we discussed Bible verses that talked about the power of the blood of Jesus. "What does Philippians 4:13 say?" I asked the students.

"I can do all things through Christ who enables me," one of the students recited.

"Good people, please talk to me and tell me what that verse means to you personally," I told the students. Many hands went up. Then I started giving them a chance one by one.

"It means that God can help me overcome lying and fighting," one student said.

"Absolutely," I said. Then I gave another student a chance.

"The verse means that God is able to help me overcome stealing and obtaining failing grades in school," he said.

On and on several students talked about the issues that caused them to be expelled from other schools and which made their parents or guardians to place them at Advent Home. They confessed their belief that God was able to overcome for them. Some students, especially the newest ones, remained quiet. My way of dealing with those ones was to give them time to listen and learn. In any case, some students who came to Advent Home confessed that they had never been to any church before. After some time, some of them were converted

God Makes a Way

and baptized.

"You are all right. God is able to overcome all those issues for us if we accept Jesus as our Savior. For those who do not know, I came here three years ago. Just like all of you, I had issues to work on. That's why God allowed me to come to Advent Home. And by God's grace, I have earned three hundred and fifty points, and I'm graduating." Every eye was now fixed on me. Even those who looked depressed that morning looked at me.

One student put up his hand and asked me, "Ms. Susan, did your parents send you here to work on your issues?"

"My parents did not sent me here, but God allowed me to come here as a teacher. Then, when I came here, I realized that I had issues that I seriously needed to work on. One of those issues was impatience. Another one was depending on my own knowledge and strength instead of depending on God. Also, I used to abuse my body by eating a lot of meat and not exercising. As a result, I was overweight and sickly. I had many more issues that I discovered when I came to Advent Home. It was not easy to overcome them, but I knew God was able to overcome for me. For three years I have been praying and working on my issues and God has overcome for me. God can overcome any issues we give Him. How many people here have anger issues?" I asked.

Almost every student put up his hand. "When I was a teenager like you, I had anger issues that made me feel like jumping out of my skin. Consequently, I used to fight both boys and girls. And I had a very bad reputation in the village. How many people have bad reputation either at home or in the neighborhood where you come from?" Many hands went up. "Okay, do you like it?" I asked.

"No," they responded.

"I didn't like my bad reputation either. Do you want to know how I got rid of my anger and the fighting spirit?" They all wanted to know my secret.

"The last time I fought I felt very bad about myself. As a result, I prayed to God to overcome that weakness for me. God answered my prayers. That's why I have never messed up anybody's dental formula here. And what do you think would have happened to me if I had punched a student's mouth because he was defiant or disrespectful?"

"You would have gone to jail," a group of students said in unison.

"True. That's why it is crucial to work on anger issues and overcome them by the power that comes from the blood of Jesus," I told them. By this time, my listeners were very motivated and receptive. The last part of our discussion had tickled them. I told them that the God who had helped me work on my issues to the point of graduation had also performed many miracles in my life. I gave them a short summary of my experience with God and how God had never let me down. I encouraged them to trust Him.

In conclusion, I asked my students, "Does anybody here want to ask God to help him overcome his issues?" Almost everyone's hands went up. I encouraged them to join a baptismal class and also read their Bibles daily and pray. We then sang *There is Power in the Blood of the Lamb* and prayed.

As I watched the students go to class that morning, my mind was fixed on my departure from Advent Home. At long last I was going to be reunited with my husband after nine long years of separation by distance. Our children were to come and join us by the end of November. I kept imagining myself cooking chapatti, stew, cabbage, or *ugali* (thick corn meal), *sukuma wiki* (kale), and bean stew with some roiko spices. I could almost smell the aroma of food fill the whole house. The last time we had all eaten together Lulu was seven years old. But now she would be a high school graduate. By mid-November, she would write her last exam to complete high school. When David left home, Wisdom was twelve years old. Now he would be twenty-one and almost finishing his undergraduate degree. I could imagine a mature discussion at the table. I could not wait to see this.

Throughout the month of August was a celebration for me and my friends at Advent Home. I had never been happier in my life. I gave testimonies and witnessed about the faithfulness of God because I was thoroughly amazed by the way He had worked to bring my family together. I always lacked the right words to thank Him. And as if that was not enough, God prepared a job for me in Texas before I could obtain employment there. In April 2010 the director of Advent Home called me to his office and told me that he was looking for people to develop online curriculum for Advent Home. He told me, "You have a master's degree is in curriculum development and instruction. Do you want to venture into a new career?"

"Sure," I said.

"Then I will get somebody to teach your subjects so that you can concentrate on the curriculum," he told me.

From the month of May onward, all I did was write curriculum. Then when I told the director I would be leaving Advent Home to go to Texas to join my family, he asked me whether I would continue writing for Advent Home from Texas. I took the offer. Later, when I considered the fact that jobs are hard to find these days, I thought this was God's providence for me. Once again, I found God very faithful. I didn't look for a job before leaving Advent Home because I was waiting to be sure that it was God's will for me to leave at that time. By the time He confirmed it, it was almost too late for me to look for a job. But God saw to it that I would not lack anything, and He provided me with a job.

However, the mood of joy and celebration about my departure changed on August 28, 2010. On that Sabbath afternoon, things seemed to take a turn for the worse.

Chapter 22

Where Are You Going From Advent Home?

On August 28, 2010, I joined the students and some staff and went to Bowman Hills Adventist Church in Tennessee where a group of our students were leading Sabbath School. I was doing the opening prayer, so I joined the students as they led song service. After the service we went back to the school. I went straight to my apartment, and after eating lunch, I listened to some music and read a little bit. Later, I took a nap. I went to sleep completely. I do not know how long I had been asleep when I was awakened by a loud voice asking, "Where are you going from Advent? Where are you going from Advent Home?"

I jumped out of bed and started speaking at once. "Why? Who is asking?" I stood in front of the dressing mirror in my bedroom and looked at myself to see if I could make out what was happening to me. My face expressed shock. I looked round the room. I was still alone in my room. The sun was shining outside, sending light streaming through the window. I looked in the mirror again and spoke loudly. "Who woke me up? Who is asking where I am going from Advent Home? Is it You, Lord? If it is You, Lord, I am going where You are leading me. If it is you, Satan, it is none of your business where I am going from here."

I felt shaken. The voice that had woken me from my sleep was loud and rough. It was a very strange voice. It was not familiar to me at all. After some time thinking, I decided to go for a prayer walk. I went to the field and started walking laps as I prayed. After walking several laps while calling upon the Lord to help me understand what had just happened, a calm voice in my head told me that Satan was not happy that my family was being reunited at last. Then the whole scenario made sense. At first, I had wondered why the Lord would ask me a question that seemed to instill doubt in my mind. All along, I believed that God was leading me. Why would He turn around at the last minute and ask me where I was going. From that time on, things were never the same again.

Well, at least I had been warned that the enemy was not happy with my blessings. Although I wished that Satan would leave me alone for once, I was used to trials and temptations. I knew where to go for help. Therefore, I deliberately intensified my prayer time and study of the Bible. That evening after the Sabbath had ended I resumed sorting out my stuff and packing. I worked until I was too tired to work anymore. The next day I woke up early in the morning with renewed strength. After my morning worship, I continued packing. Suddenly, my cell phone rang. I picked it and started talking without actually looking to see who the caller was. It was David. However, his first sentence told me that he was upset with me.

"Why haven't you been taking my calls?" he asked.

"I did not hear any call since last night. When did you call?" I asked him.

"Just check your phone and see how many missed calls you have," he told me.

"I'm very sorry. But I want you to know that I have no reason to ignore your calls. Since last night I have been working between upstairs and downstairs. Maybe you called when I was away from my phone. My mind is focused on packing and cleaning the apartment. I did not bother with my phone," I told him.

David had called me the previous evening when I was doing my prayer walk. We had talked briefly and had agreed that we would talk the next day. Apparently, he had called me late in the evening, but I did not hear the phone ring. Again, on Sunday morning he had called me several times while I was washing and blow-drying my hair in the bathroom. All the same, I did not understand why he should be that upset. Later that day he called me again and asked me when I had last talked to our son. I told him I did not remember the exact day. It was some time the previous week. I asked him whether he had talked with him. Again, he did not take my question well. Then we got into an argument and more misunderstandings.

Then I started thinking. *What is happening to David? For a long time we have not quarreled. Why is he getting so upset over nothing? What is bothering him? Is he anxious about me coming to live with him? He has always been pushing me to move to Texas and be with him. Should I change my mind and either go elsewhere or renew my contract with Advent Home? My services are still needed at Advent Home.*

These thoughts were interrupted by the very clear calm voice that had told me that Satan was not happy about my family being reunited. It was then that I came to my senses. I realized that the devil was fighting us. I prayed for strength to hang on to my faith no matter what happened. And to my encouragement, our communication improved later in the week when I asked David, "What's happening to you, darling? Are you scared of me coming to live with you permanently?"

"No. Not at all. The only other time I was this excited about us staying together was when I was going to marry you. I am looking forward to the day you will wake up in this apartment. My problem in the beginning of this week was that I thought you were ignoring me and making me miserable for no reason. Every time I called you, before I could find you, my mind told me that you were just ignoring me," he said.

"Why would I do that?' I asked.

"I don't know. And I know that's really unlike you, but I was just getting so frustrated," he responded.

"I want you to know that Satan is not happy about our reunion. Pray like you have never prayed before," I told him.

"Oh! Okay, I am going to pray, but don't worry about Satan. He is a defeated foe," he told me.

"Thank you for your encouragement," I said.

Then David asked me how much luggage I had. He told me he wanted to book the vehicle we were going to use for my transportation. I told him I had quite a lot. He promised to take a big car.

I continued working during the day and packing in the evenings. On Thursday, the last week of August, somebody called me and told me that I was needed at the main building of the organization. The caller told me to make sure I was there at 6:30 p.m. I looked at my watch and realized that I had one hour to take my books from my office to my apartment. A colleague went with me to my office to help me put the heavy cartons in the trunk of her car. We loaded two cartons and took them to the apartment.

Upon parking in front of my apartment, I got out of the car and proceeded to take the heavy cartons out of the trunk. I told my colleague not to come out. I said I could manage. I took the two cartons out of the car. However, as I closed the trunk door, I did not take my hand out quickly enough. So as I shut the trunk, my little finger was caught and crushed. The only thing I saw was blood, and for a moment I thought the nail was cut in two. The pain I felt made me sweat all over my body. I could not remember the last time I had experienced that kind of pain.

My colleague rushed me to the main building of the organization to treat me. As I received first aid, it dawned on me that the organization had organized a cake eating function for both students and staff for my farewell. People soon came around looking for me wondering why I was taking so long to be with them at the function. Unfortunately, at that time pain sparks were still rushing from the nail to my armpit.

Anyway, I quietly prayed to God to apply His balm on me to ease the pain, and I went out to join my colleagues and students. As soon as I sat down, the school choir started singing an African religious song. Although I did not understand the language, I got excited. I was given a piece of cake and a cup of juice. I did not think I could swallow anything. My body was in shock. But apart from about three people who knew what had happened to me, the rest did not know what I was going through. They continued addressing me and hugging me. I managed a smile.

I was still confused by the pain and thoughts about what exactly was happening to me when the director called me to the front of the gathering. In his hand he held an emblem (a wall hanging gift) for me. Then he started reading the writing on it.

"Presented to Mrs. Susan Mbaluka.

"In appreciation of your support as an Educator and Spiritual Mentor to the students of Advent Home."

He continued to read the second paragraph.

"There is no limit to the usefulness of one who, putting self aside, makes room for the working of the Holy Spirit upon [her] heart, and lives a life wholly consecrated to God" (Ellen G. White, *Our High Calling*, p. 151).

Thank you, may God bless you!
Advent Home Learning Center, Inc.
Established 1985."

As students and staff clapped, I felt as if I was hearing it all from a distance. However, my smile did not fail me. I thanked everybody for the surprise. If only they knew that Satan had also surprised me. My spirit remained strong. I knew what was happening. It was not the first time I had experienced the controversy between good and evil. I was used to it now. All I had to do was hold on to my Lord and never give up. The organization's surprise was very sweet. I loved the gift they gave me. I had always wanted to be associated with God's work. So whenever I looked at the gift, my pain felt a bit numb. By the time I finished greeting and hugging my students, colleagues, and friends, it was almost 8:00 p.m.

David was coming the following day, Friday, September 3, 2010. We would go to church and spend the Sabbath at Advent Home. We planned to leave in the wee hours of Sunday morning, September 5. However, three days before Friday, David told me that he was not feeling very well. Therefore, he asked a friend to come with him to help him with the twelve-hour drive from Texas to Tennessee.

Although I was in pain and one hand could not touch anything for hours, I was done with most of my packing. David could help me with whatever was remaining. I called and told him all that had happened to me. He panicked and wanted me to go to the hospital, but I told him I was fine. He could not wait to come and see me the next day. We talked and reviewed all our plans. Everything was going well apart from the fact that he had been sick the whole week and still felt weak and dizzy. But we hoped he would get better, and in any case his friend would do much of the driving, especially during their trip to Tennessee, hoping that by Sunday, on our way to Texas, David would be well enough to help his friend drive. We wished each other a good night, hoping to meet the next day.

However, two hours later, David called and told me that his friend had just called him and told him that he had been called to go to work the following day. Therefore, the friend could not accompany David to Tennessee.

"What are we going to do?" I asked.

"I will come for you. I will come alone," David said.

"You are weak and dizzy. You cannot drive twelve hours in that condition,"

I told him.

"Let's pray that by tomorrow morning I will be well," he said.

"Okay, let's talk tomorrow morning and see how you are feeling," we agreed.

The next day David still felt very dizzy and weak.

"I will come and take breaks on the way," David told me.

"No. Don't try it. I will come on my own," I told him.

"What are you going to do? You cannot drive a long distance yourself?" he asked.

"I am going to fly," I said.

"What about the luggage?" he asked.

"I will send it by bus or by mail, whichever is cheaper," I told him.

"Okay, I am going to buy the air ticket for you. When do you want to come?" he asked.

"Wait until I send the luggage. Then I will tell you when to book the flight," I said.

I told David to relax and not to worry about me. I was in God's hands, and I would be fine. However, I felt lost. First of all, a new employee was to take my apartment immediately I left. I did not have a car to take my luggage to a location from which it would be sent to Texas. I prayed and asked God for wisdom on how to deal with my situation.

Friday evening came, and the Sabbath began. This was my last Sabbath at Advent Home. The school choir was going to Collegedale Community Church where they would sing a Swahili song. Both the students and the choir leader invited me to go with them since I would be almost the only one who could understand the Swahili song.

I joined the choir to church. After the service we went to a park near Southern Adventist University and ate our packed lunch. Then we went for a walk. At around 4:00 p.m. we went back to Advent Home. All this time I refused to stress about what I was going to do with my luggage. After Sabbath was over, I started unpacking so as to repack one suitcase and a handbag to take with me on the plane. In addition, I had to pack all the other suitcases and cartons differently to fit public transportation. Now that my little finger was hurting, it was very frustrating for me to pack things again. As I went through all this, I kept wondering, *Why did David have to get sick at this time? Why did his friend fail at the last minute? Why did I have to hurt my finger when I needed to pack and clean the apartment? Why did God allow all this to happen.*

On Saturday evening a thought came to my mind. I decided to call my friend Josephine and tell her what was happening to me. She and her husband had a van that could take all of my luggage at once. Josephine and her husband, Ken, were glad to help me. On Monday evening Ken came with his cousin and took me together with my luggage to their house in Chattanooga. Meanwhile, David urged me to book a flight because the longer I waited the higher the price would be. I told him to book me a flight from Atlanta. He searched, but he could not get a flight that we could afford from Atlanta. Finally, he found one from Nashville. Now that my flight was secured, I concentrated on searching for means to send my luggage from Chattanooga to Houston, Texas.

To my disappointment, every alternative was too expensive. I would need a few thousand dollars to ship all of my luggage. I decided that I would leave my luggage somewhere, and then pick it up when David was well. Josephine and Ken could not keep the stuff for me because they did not have the space. The only place I could leave my stuff was at my sister and brother-in-law's place in Nashville. I called my sister-in-law, Agnes, and asked her whether she could keep my luggage for me.

"Sure. We have plenty of room. I'm sure your luggage cannot even fill the space we have in our house," she told me. Then Ken and his cousin took me and my luggage to Nashville.

Later, I looked back and remembered that David and I wanted so badly to get a flight from Atlanta, but we couldn't find any. When it happened that I had to take my luggage to Nashville where I had booked my flight, I saw God's hand leading me behind the scenes. If I had booked the flight from Atlanta, it would have been very frustrating for me to take my luggage to Nashville and then have to go back to Chattanooga that night so that I could travel to Atlanta to catch my flight early in the morning the next day.

I shared my thoughts with Josephine. Then she told me, "Susana, God loves you so much. Do you know the van that Ken used to carry your luggage had been broken down for a very long time. We just got it repaired a day before you called us to transport you. Then look at the way God organized your trip. God knew that you would have to take your luggage to Nashville. So He did not provide a flight for you in Atlanta because that would have been tiresome."

"Do you know all the time I have been unpacking and repacking my luggage because David could not come for me, I have been praying, 'God, please help me,'" I said.

"God has been with you all the time because you are the first person to use the van since it was repaired," she told me.

In Nashville, my in-laws, Agnes and Samuel, received us very well. We unloaded my luggage and after eating supper, Ken and his cousin went back to Chattanooga. Agnes, Samuel, and I spent almost half the night talking. We had a great time catching up. The next day they dropped me off at the airport on their way to work. As I waited to board the flight to Houston, I felt numb. I did not know what to think about myself or what had been happening in the last two weeks. All the same, the only thing I wanted this side of heaven was to set my eyes on David. I wanted to go and take care of him.

By 1:00 p.m. I landed at Bush International Airport in Houston. I found David waiting for me. Although his face looked pale from the stomach problems he had been fighting and from not eating well, he gave me a big smile and a warm hug.

When we reached his apartment, I knew that God had overcome all that the devil had planned. David and I worshipped and thanked God for bringing us together after what had seemed like forever. Then I told David, "We need to pray all the time. Satan worked so hard to prevent me from coming to join you. I wonder why he is fighting our reunion so hard. I am here now, by God's grace, but I don't think Satan will leave us alone for long. Whatever his plans may be, God is with us. Let us keep vigilant in prayer."

We read from Ephesians 6:16-18: "Above all, taking the shield of faith, wherewith ye shall be able to quench all the fiery darts of the wicked. And take the helmet of salvation, and the sword of the Spirit, which is the word of God: Praying always with all prayer and supplication in the Spirit, and watching thereunto with all perseverance and supplication for all saints."

From this point on, the journey for the two of us had begun all over again.

Chapter 23

Reunited at Last

After praying and thanking God for bringing me safely to David, we paid attention to each other. "Dave, why are you looking so emaciated?" I asked.

"I have been sick, and I've also been very stressed because of what you have been going through. I felt very bad that I could not come for you. And I have not been eating well at all. I have just been swallowing some things so that I can stay alive. Separation from family is a very bad thing," he said.

"That separation was one of the worst things that has ever happened to us," I said.

"Let me give you something to eat," he said.

"What do you have here? I know you have not been cooking," I said.

"You are right, but you can't miss something to eat," he responded.

"I'll take a quick shower as you get the food ready," I said as I entered the bathroom. When I came to the dining table shortly afterward, I found *ugali* (thick cornmeal), spinach, and beans. The food was delicious.

"I like the way you cook your *ugali*. When you mix the corn flour with whole wheat flour, you make your *ugali* very nutritious," I told him.

"When your wife runs away from you, you must learn survival techniques," he teased.

"This wife didn't run away. She kept running after her husband," I told him.

"That's why I love you so much, and I so much thank God for you. I am a blessed man," he said.

"Yes, indeed you are a blessed man," I agreed with a teasing tone.

"And are you a blessed woman?" he asked.

"A little bit," I said as I watched his face. We both burst out laughing. "Seriously, yes. I am a blessed woman. If I were to look for a husband all over again, I would still choose you. I respect the fact that, though we have all been separated by distance, you have called the children at least once every week for those nine years. You did the same with me when I was in Kenya, and since I came to the U.S., you have made sure that we talked every day even if it was for five minutes. In addition, for all those years, if you didn't have your morals right, you would have children with other women. Or could you be having some little Lulus and Wisdoms somewhere in Texas?" I asked.

"If I did you would have known the minute they were born. The animal known as child support in the U.S. is no joke. And it is hard to keep it a secret. Once in a while you may be required to spend time with your son or daughter," he told me.

"I know. And all I can say is that God is good, and He has been very gracious to us. I do not have the right words to thank Him for His mercies to us. I cannot believe that in two months' time, God willing, we will have our children here," I said.

"Even before then, I don't know how to thank God for just having you in this apartment. I have stayed alone for nine years. If you notice, I don't talk the way I used to. I have been quiet for so long. When I go to work, I talk to people, but that's not much because everybody is busy doing his thing. When I come home from work, I am too lonely to cook and eat. In most cases, I just eat something when I feel too hungry to move on," he said.

"That's not good for your health," I said

We had a few things to adjust to here and there. First of all, we had to rearrange things, especially in the bedroom to accommodate me. David gladly cooperated and created space for me. Also, I asked him whether he minded me rearranging things in the kitchen and in the living room.

"No, no. This is your apartment now. Do with it as you see fit. Whenever you need my help to move something, let me know," he said.

Within a few days, we were able to organize our living room in a better way. "Look at how beautiful the house is! Blessed is the man who finds a good wife," David said.

"I think more blessed is a woman who finds a good husband," I responded.

As time went by, David and I became more attached to each other. He would go to work, and I would remain in the apartment working on Advent Home curriculum. Now that I was at home, this gave me a chance to spend as much time with David as possible whenever he was not at work.

Then I had a flashback and remembered how frustrated I had been two months before when I realized I had to postpone pursuing my doctorate in school administration. Andrews University had admitted me to start my program in July 2010. I really wanted to start, but I realized that there was too much going on in my life around that time. I needed to move from Advent Home to Texas; I had just started a new career of curriculum development, which was more demanding than teaching; and David and I needed to put together every coin we had to move our children from Kenya to the U.S. and help them get settled. Once the children came to the U.S., they would need my attention, especially for the first few months. I realized I was at the center of all this, and if on top of working, I started taking classes, I would either have to drop out of school or ignore my family when they needed me most.

I chose to suspend the school to get the family together before anything else. Although I knew this was the best thing to do, I still wished it was possible to start my studies. Later, I was very grateful to God that He did not let me have my wish. At least I had some time to cook for my husband and spend time with him on our second honeymoon as we prepared to receive our children.

Two weeks after I arrived in Houston, there was a special prayer day at the church David attended, West Houston SDA Church. The pastor announced that that Sabbath evening, from 7:00 p.m. to 10:00 p.m., would be dedicated to prayer. People were asked to go and pray for their needs and the needs of their friends and families. Also, people would get a chance to give thanks to God for anything the Lord had done for them. David and I attended this special prayer function. We all got a chance to give our requests to God in a very special way. Then came the time to give testimonies and thanks to God for the good things He had done for His people. Quite a number of people put their hands up to give their testimonies. My hand went up, too.

When at last I was given the chance to speak, I briefly introduced myself and told the church, "Mine is a testimony about God's faithfulness. My husband and I have been separated by distance for nine years. For those nine years, I have been praying to God to sustain my marriage. My husband was in Texas all this time. I was in Kenya for nearly six years, and for three years, I have been in Tennessee. I refused to give up on my marriage, and I kept praying to God to make a way for my family to be reunited. While I have been in Tennessee and my husband in Texas, our children have been in Kenya. I knew it would take the hand of God to bring our family together because there were visas involved.

"In short, I want you to know that God has been performing one miracle after another for my family to come together. First of all, He miraculously gave me a teaching job in Tennessee, which allowed me to come straight from my village in Kenya to teach in the U.S. Secondly, within a year, God gave me a green card at a time when it was extremely hard for R1 visa holders to get green cards. Lastly, God gave my children visas to come to the U.S. by December this year so that they too could get their green cards. Two weeks ago I left Tennessee to come and live with my husband here in Houston. Before December this year, we expect our children to be here to complete the family reunion.

"I have found God to be incredibly faithful. And He has power to perform any miracle for any of His children according to His will. Tonight we are gathered here to give our requests to God. Whatever your needs are, 'trust in the Lord and He will give you the desires of your heart.' I have tested Him, and I have found Him true. Just imagine what is happening in the institution of marriage today. And imagine a husband and a wife separated by distance for nine years. God sustained our marriage for that long. Trust the God of heaven, and He will do the same for you, according to His will." I sat down as the church echoed with amen.

On the next Sabbath, several people came to talk to me and to ask me more questions about my life experience. This gave me more opportunities to witness for God, for all His goodness to me. I encouraged people to trust God with their financial, social, spiritual, and health needs. Nothing made me as happy as the testimony God had given me. Given a chance, I would repeat it over and over again throughout my life.

To the reader of this book, I encourage you to trust God with your life. He will never fail you.

In conclusion, whichever way I look at God, I find Him worthy of my love and my worship because of His faithfulness and His love for me and for all His other children.

All I ask of Him is to increase my faith and trust in Him and to give me the grace to do His will so that when Jesus comes back He will find me ready to go with Him to heaven.

I pray that you will experience God's love and salvation through Jesus Christ.

We invite you to view the complete
selection of titles we publish at:

www.TEACHServices.com

Scan with your mobile
device to go directly
to our website.

Please write or email us your praises, reactions, or
thoughts about this or any other book we publish at:

TEACH Services, Inc.
P U B L I S H I N G

www.TEACHServices.com

P.O. Box 954
Ringgold, GA 30736

info@TEACHServices.com

TEACH Services, Inc., titles may be purchased in bulk for
educational, business, fund-raising, or sales promotional use.
For information, please e-mail:

BulkSales@TEACHServices.com

Finally, if you are interested in seeing
your own book in print, please contact us at

publishing@TEACHServices.com

We would be happy to review your manuscript for free.

www.ingramcontent.com/pod-product-compliance
Lightning Source LLC
Chambersburg PA
CBHW021921180426
43200CB00027B/208